DARKNESS
WILL NOT OVERCOME

DARKNESS
WILL NOT OVERCOME

ONE PERSON'S STRUGGLE AND RECOVERY FROM OPIOIDS

RICHIE HALVERSEN

Pacific Press® Publishing Association
Nampa, Idaho | www.pacificpress.com

Cover design by Steve Lanto
Cover design resources from iStockphoto.com | 1065002186

Copyright © 2019 by Pacific Press® Publishing Association
Printed in the United States of America
All rights reserved

The author assumes full responsibility for the accuracy of all facts and quotations as cited in this book.

Unless otherwise noted, Scripture quotations are from The Holy Bible, English Standard Version® (ESV®), copyright © 2001 by Crossway, a publishing ministry of Good News Publishers. Used by permission. All rights reserved.

Scripture quotations marked NIV are from THE HOLY BIBLE, NEW INTERNATIONAL VERSION®. Copyright © 1973, 1978, 1984, 2011 by Biblica, Inc.® Used by permission. All rights reserved worldwide.

Scripture quotations marked NLT are taken from the Holy Bible, New Living Translation, copyright © 1996, 2004, 2007, 2013, 2015 by Tyndale House Foundation. Used by permission of Tyndale House Publishers, Inc., Carol Stream, Illinois 60188. All rights reserved.

Additional copies of this book are available by calling toll-free 1-800-765-6955 or by visiting AdventistBookCenter.com.

Library of Congress Cataloging-in-Publication Data

Names: Halversen, Richie, author.
Title: Darkness will not overcome : one person's struggle and recovery from opioids / Richie Halversen.
Description: Nampa : Pacific Press Publishing Association, 2019.
Identifiers: LCCN 2019019059 | ISBN 9780816365265 (pbk. : alk. paper)
Subjects: LCSH: Halversen, Richie. | Drug addicts—Religious life. |
  Substance abuse—Religious aspects—Christianity. | Opioid abuse—Biography.
Classification: LCC BV4596.A24 H35 2019 | DDC 248.8/6293092 [B] —dc23 LC
  record available at https://lccn.loc.gov/2019019059

September 2019

Dedication

To God: Thank you for never giving up on me. My beautiful wife, Brittney: thank you for remaining committed to me. To my four children: I love you more than you know. My parents: thank you for the love, prayers, and support. And to my sisters: thank you for your strength, courage, and faith in God.

Contents

Foreword		9
Chapter 1	The Beginning	13
Chapter 2	A Downward Spiral	16
Chapter 3	The Con	23
Chapter 4	A Visit to Church	27
Chapter 5	Trouble at Kmart	30
Chapter 6	Twin Falls	40
Chapter 7	Connecting Flight	49
Chapter 8	Upside Down on a Bridge and in My Marriage	53
Chapter 9	Christmas Alone	58
Chapter 10	Gooding, Idaho	61
Chapter 11	The Crucible of Withdrawal	71
Chapter 12	The Ropes Course	75
Chapter 13	Family Day	80
Chapter 14	Give and You Shall Receive	85
Chapter 15	Graduation	91
Chapter 16	Reunions	97
Chapter 17	Recovery	102
Chapter 18	Judgment Day	107
Chapter 19	Making Amends	114
Chapter 20	New Life	119
Chapter 21	Preacher Man	122
Chapter 22	The Darkness Will Not Overcome	126

Foreword

God has many ways to transform lives. This story is about how He transformed me. I share it to give people hope. God never gives up on us. This book can be broken down into two parts: my problem and His solution. I share the problem not to bring attention to it. In recovery, people called them "war stories." When people start telling "war stories" in a meeting, a good facilitator will interrupt and gently, or not so gently, remind people, "let's get out of the problem and into the solution." Focusing on the problem never helps anyone. It only hurts. I share on the problem not to tell a "war story" but to help you see where my addiction took me. And more importantly to show what God rescued me from. I share everything—the good, the bad, and the ugly in order to give hope. If God was able to change my life, He can change yours, or the life of someone you love.

I believe one of the greatest threats to our communities and families is addiction. Everyone has been hurt by it. Either you struggle with it, or you know someone who does. We are living in an opioid crisis. "Every day, more than 130 people in the United States die after overdosing on opioids."[1]

What do we know about the opioid crises?

- Roughly 21 to 29 percent of patients prescribed opioids

for chronic pain misuse them.
- Between 8 and 12 percent develop an opioid use disorder.
- An estimated 4 to 6 percent who misuse prescription opioids transition to heroin.
- About 80 percent of people who use heroin first misused prescription opioids.
- Opioid overdoses increased 30 percent from July 2016 through September 2017 in 52 areas in 45 states.
- The Midwestern region saw opioid overdoses increase 70 percent from July 2016 through September 2017.
- Opioid overdoses in large cities increased by 54 percent in 16 states.[2]

The good news however is there is hope. In this book, I tell the story of how I got clean and how I have stayed clean. I could not have done it if it was not for God, my church, and a fellowship of recovering addicts. I do not believe my way is the only way. Jesus is the only way. However, recovery requires treatment. If positive changes aren't made, nothing will change. Recovery means getting honest with others and with yourself—especially yourself. Recovery doesn't just happen or take place overnight. It requires a lifetime of prayer, patience, and persistence. The local church has been a vital component to my recovery, but very seldom can a church handle all the issues that arise during the recovery process. Most churches are just not set up to address all of the different aspects of addiction. However, I am hoping one of the results of this book is to open the eyes of church and civic leaders who will in turn help create communities of recovery.

There hasn't been a program that has helped more people with addiction than The Twelve Steps of Alcoholics Anonymous. From Alcoholics Anonymous (AA) many other twelve-step groups have emerged: Narcotics Anonymous, Overeaters Anonymous,

Foreword

and Celebrate Recovery, and many more have helped thousands of addicts get clean and stay clean. Twelve-step programs provide the honesty, safety, autonomy, and accountability addicts need to recover. You can abstain from substances and still not recover. Drug use is only a symptom of a much larger problem. Real recovery starts with abstinence, but it doesn't end there. The addict must work through the steps of a program that will get to the heart of the problem.

In the book of Joel, the prophet describes a scourge of locusts. To which he says,

> Tell your children of it,
>   and let your children tell their children,
>   and their children to another generation.
> What the cutting locust left,
>   the swarming locust has eaten.
> What the swarming locust left,
>   the hopping locust has eaten,
> and what the hopping locust left,
>   the destroying locust has eaten (Joel 1:3, 4).

Just as this plague left nothing and ate everything, so it is with addiction. It continues to take and take and take until there is nothing left to take. But we serve a God who can restore what the locusts have eaten. I can't, He can, I think I'll let Him.

Here are some resources you might check out if you, or someone you love, is struggling with addiction:

- Alcoholics, Anonymous, visit https://www.aa.org
- Narcotics Anonymous, visit https://www.na.org
- Celebrate Recovery, visit https://www.celebraterecovery.com
- National Institute on Drug Abuse, visit https://www.drugabuse.gov or call 301-443-1124.

Darkness Will Not Overcome

- National Institute on Alcohol Abuse and Alcoholism, visit https://www.niaaa.nih.gov or call 301-443-3860.

---

1. "Opioid Overdose Crisis," National Institute on Drug Abuse, revised January 2019, https://www.drugabuse.gov/drugs-abuse/opioids/opioid-overdose-crisis.
2. "Opioid Overdose Crisis."

Chapter 1

The Beginning

"Do you want to be a preacher like your father when you grow up?" The old lady smelled of mothballs and peppermints. The light coming in through the stained glass obscured the woman's face. She stood in just the right place for the outline of her head to glow like a little sun.

The church service had just finished. My father had assumed his usual post after preaching—standing at the door shaking hands with people as they left the sanctuary. Being the son of a pastor comes with drawbacks, particularly that you're always on display. It seemed as though the *appearance* was more important than the *person*. They wanted you to be the model family—whether you were that or not didn't really matter. The appearance was all that mattered. At least, that was how it felt sometimes. After each service, we had to stand near my father to receive or respond to the various comments and questions that would be directed our way. People tended to ask the same questions, uninteresting questions that really didn't want a response: "How's school?" "How is your year?" "How was your summer?" and the most popular one I got: "Do you want to be a preacher when you grow up?" They didn't treat other kids like this—just the pastor's kids. As if we're supposed to be model kids, from model families, made available

Darkness Will Not Overcome

for them to gawk at like some sort of holy exhibition. At a young age, I realized that many of the people who asked me questions weren't looking for my answer; instead, they were looking for the answer they thought I should give. So I gave them the answers I thought they were looking for. All the people weren't fake. As with anything, there are good, genuine people in the church, and there are those who may mean well but are not genuine.

Being a pastor's kid wasn't all bad. In fact, for years, I loved it. I loved being a part of something that seemed bigger than me. It was exciting to feel a sense of mission. It was a life that, at times, seemed larger than the usual situation of working a job, buying a house, having a family. There were many success stories in the church, stories of people's lives that had changed for the better.

The old lady continued staring at me. She gave me the look old ladies like to give adolescent boys—the kind of look they give you right before they reach out and pinch your cheek. I was fourteen—certainly too old for the old-lady cheek pinch—but I could tell she was thinking it.

Do you want to be a preacher like your father when you grow up? Her question echoed in my mind. My answer to that question up until a year or so previous would have been an enthusiastic yes, but now it had become an energetic no. The spell of wanting to do whatever your father does when you grow up had dissipated. With age and an increasingly cynical outlook, I came to resent the question. I wanted to be my own person. I didn't want to be God's property or the church's property. I wanted to be my own property. I wanted to do my own thing.

"I don't think so." I forced a small smile.

"Well, that's too bad. If you're anything like your father, that would be a real waste." She walked away. The stained-glass halo disappeared with her. The smell of mothballs and peppermints stayed behind.

Yeah, well, no thanks, I thought, with a plastic smile on my face as I watched her leave.

The Beginning

I held back from the large group accumulating near where my father was and started moving toward the back of the church, where I could slip out one of the side doors undetected. My feet moved as quickly as they could on the wine-colored carpet. I could feel the eyes of the stained-glass Jesus staring at me as I walked by. He was keeping watch over His stained-glass sheep—but I was positive that He was looking at me, too, His expression a contradiction of gentle indifference. It haunted me. It was a look that cared—just not enough to do anything about it. To me, it was a look that said, "You better get your act together, Richie, and hurry along with the rest of the sheep." But I didn't want to be a sheep. Sheep are stupid. Sheep are unoriginal. Sheep seemed so insignificant. I wanted more!

I breathed a sigh of relief when I reached the dark hallway in the back of the church. The unease of the stained-glass stare dissipated. The exit sign beckoned to me through the darkness, inviting me to escape. I would wait for my family at the usual spot, under the giant oak tree where our car was always parked. That was my refuge after church. For the past year, I had escaped to that spot as soon as services were over. Or as soon as I thought I had made enough of an appearance not to get a lecture from my parents when we got home. Once I got to the giant oak, I could breathe a sigh of relief. I no longer felt like I had to perform. I could just be myself—sitting on the grass with my back against the big tree, daydreaming of what my life could be.

CHAPTER 2

A Downward Spiral

The sound of a semitruck passing startled me awake. I slammed the brakes as hard as I could. It felt as though the car were crashing; the wheel wasn't working. Why wasn't the car turning? Until after a few panic-soaked seconds of screaming, it dawned on me—the car wasn't moving. Suddenly I remembered pulling over onto the shoulder. Exhausted, I had fallen asleep. It felt like forever, but it had only been a few minutes.

I had been driving all day and most of the night, which had become a frequent activity for me. Driving to hospitals I had never been to, going to see doctors I had not yet seen—which I was quickly running out of—each day driving farther than I had the day before, at times driving as far as two hundred miles for just one prescription. Just a handful of highs. There were a few days I was lucky and scored on the first stop, and I could call it a day. But most days were like today, stopping at four or five different places before I got enough drugs to take a break—at least until the next morning. My addiction had grown, quietly, persistently. It went, seemingly overnight, from fun recreation to a full-time job. It had become a relentless taskmaster, striking its whip, constantly riding me for more.

The night was hot and humid, my car unbearably stuffy. I

started the car to get the air conditioning going, looking in my rearview mirror. I was constantly paranoid. I don't know what I was thinking, pulling over on the shoulder like this. What would've happened if a police officer pulled over and I answered his questions wrong or, worse, he decided to search my car?

I felt my pockets with the usual panic. The reassuring shape of a pill bottle eased the anxiety a little. Darvocet. Man, I hated Darvocet. It was better than nothing, but not much. You couldn't just ask for the drug you wanted. If you did, it put a flashing neon sign above your head: "junkie," "addict," "drug seeker." No, you had to pretend that you didn't know the difference between hydrocodone and aspirin, even though addicts probably know as much, if not more, than your local pharmacist.

At times, the desperation was enough that you let down your guard, and they would send you away with a prescription of Tramadol or Darvocet, the kind of painkiller they give you when they want to get rid of you, when they're suspicious of drug use but not sure enough to give you nothing. There were times I think the doctors just had pity on me. They saw through the charade from the beginning. They just wanted to get rid of me. Or maybe they were themselves addicts, and they saw the desperation in my eyes and could relate, so helped me out a little. That was rare. They were too busy finding ways and means to get their own dope.

I shifted the car into drive and headed back in the direction of home. Sunrise was just a few hours away. I was hoping I could get home before my wife woke up, before she realized I had been gone all night. That wouldn't be good. Our relationship was struggling already. Arguments were increasing every day. Trust was eroding away like my sanity.

Hoping I would earn some points, I went to church with my wife and the kids the other day. I didn't mind church so much. I had never had a hard time believing in the existence of God, even when my life was in the toilet. In fact, addiction had only confirmed my conviction that we are spiritual creatures. We were made to worship. If we don't worship God, we will worship something else. My using had become my worship.

With each high, I tried to take a shortcut to heaven, hoping for those pain-free days, bowing down at the altar of an endorphin rush, going from one high to the next, trying to encapsulate a feeling, a freedom, a peace, and stretching it into eternity. What is that if not worship? Everything we do seems to have this in the background. I don't care what it is. Drug addiction, alcoholism, workaholism, materialism—got to get the new car, the new weight, the new high—all desperate attempts to grasp for something that is always just out of reach, looking for someone, or something, that can make the pain go away.

The problem was that the higher I started getting, the harder I started falling. The closer I got to heaven, the more my life started resembling hell. The more I tried to put my pieces back together again, the more broken I became. That's the downside of being an addict. Eventually, you always have to come back down. The very thing you're using to make you whole again is secretly siphoning your soul away, each time taking another piece of you until there's nothing left to take.

I rubbed my tongue over the empty socket in my mouth, where my tooth once was. It was getting so bad I was giving up teeth. A few days before, I had one pulled for some pills. I had gone to a dentist in Kentucky and given him the usual toothache story. I had become an expert in exhibiting all the classic symptoms of an abscessed tooth, each time getting better at what I should and shouldn't say. But this guy saw through me from the beginning. No "here's an antibiotic and painkiller, come back in a few days"; of course, I would never come back. The only thing this guy kept pushing was to pull the tooth.

"If it hurts, we can pull the tooth," he said plainly. What kind of backwoods dentist had I happened upon?

"Isn't there something else we can do? I'd rather not—"

A Downward Spiral

"Nope," he said, cutting me off. "This is your only choice."

"What about a root canal?" I asked, for a second realizing how ridiculous I was getting. You know you're bad off when you're asking for root canals.

"I don't do root canals," he said. Sometimes you hit a home run, and sometimes you strike out. I had a feeling this was a strikeout. "I'll pull the tooth. Give you some painkillers, and you should be good."

Well, that's all he had to say for my tooth to be as good as gone. This dentist had fit me in at the end of his day. I had already been to two doctors before this one and gotten nothing. My door was closing quickly. *It's just one molar*, I thought to myself. *I can get an implant or bridge later on.* This is what addiction does. It causes temporary lapses of sanity. Getting a tooth pulled for a dozen pills I would blow through in a few hours?

"OK, go ahead and pull it," I said.

As I was driving back home, tonguing the empty socket in my mouth, reality came crashing in. What an idiot. All of that for Darvocet? I hate Darvocet!

There had to be an easier way than this. Losing teeth—really? I only had so many teeth to go around. Jumping from doctor to doctor, from emergency room to emergency room, I had so many medical bills that my bills had bills. There was no way I'd ever be able to crawl out of the debt I had created over the last few years. Plus, my tolerance levels were rising to the point that there were not enough hours in the day to get the number of prescriptions I needed just to get by. I had to figure something else out.

An idea continued entering my mind. Up to this point, I pushed it out as quickly as it came in, but I was reaching the point where I had to consider it. How many times had I heard doctors call in a prescription? How many times had I studied the little slip of paper before taking it to the pharmacy? How hard could it be to call in my own prescriptions? I mean, they put the

Darkness Will Not Overcome

DEA number right on the paper.

I rehearsed it in my mind: *Hello, this is Doctor _____; I have a prescription to call in. The patient's name is Richie Halversen, Lortab ten, take every four to six hours p.r.n., DEA number is*—I mean, how hard was that?

The more I thought about it and rehearsed it, the more I became convinced I could do it. Sure, deep down, I knew I would probably get caught. But I didn't care. In addiction, you become so good at lying that you actually start believing your own lies. Lies are easier than the truth. Suddenly you find yourself in places you swore you would never go and doing things you swore you would never do. It's easier to believe in a lie than to admit the truth. I remember all the promises I had made growing up. "I'll never do that . . ." I was breaking every single one of those promises.

Just the other day I broke one. I swore I would never be one of "those people" who beg for money. Growing up in the tourist town of Nashville, I was used to panhandlers coming up to me and asking me for money. I had heard every story, and variation, there was. I had promised I would never be one of "those people." But I had run out of money. And when dope is involved, all bets are off.

My two kids were with me. Kaleb was four; Hayley, one. I was hoping my kids would validate my story or at least cause someone to pity me. Addiction makes everyone a means to get high. Nothing is sacred except for getting high.

I walked into a small restaurant and gave one of the stories I swore I would never tell.

"I've run out of gas. I need to get my kids home." I was met with immediate suspicion. I guess I didn't look as convincing as I thought I did.

The guy looked at me with a sad expression and said, "Sorry, sir, we don't give away money here. This is a restaurant. If you need some food, we can help you and your kids with that."

A Downward Spiral

"We don't need food. Just some gas to get us home. Please, just a few dollars," I begged, showcasing my two children to try to break through this guy's resolve.

"Sorry, man," he said.

I left the restaurant, the shame strong, the addiction stronger. I was walking to my car when I heard someone shout behind me.

"Hey, buddy." It was the guy from the restaurant.

"I'm giving this to you because of your kids. I don't know if you're legit or not. I hope you are, but if you're not, that's on you, not me." He handed me a twenty-dollar bill. "If you're not legit, man, get some help. Don't put your children in this position."

"I promise, it's the truth." Lies. "Thank you so much. I really appreciate this. I promise I will pay you back," I said as he continued to look at me with a pitiful stare.

"That would be nice," he said.

"I will."

"Good luck, man," he said as he turned away.

I had sworn I would never beg for money, no matter how bad it got. But the begging and the conning and the manipulating would only continue to get worse, more common, and more desperate. Once you say yes to one lie, it becomes easier and easier to say yes to other lies. You keep sinking to a place where nothing becomes off-limits. You start becoming someone else entirely, someone you would barely recognize if you actually took the time to look at yourself in the mirror. Every day I became more and more accustomed to my new self. The old Richie was becoming a stranger I didn't know.

Before doing anything illegal, you start selling your possessions one by one. Your favorite CDs, your kid's DVDs, the watch your grandfather gave you, or that ring you've been wearing since you said, "I do." Suddenly stuff isn't as important as it was, at least not as important as getting high. I had gone from lifting money from a family member's wallet to borrowing money "one last time," to now begging for it, making promises to pay it back with no intention of ever paying anything back. "If only I could get enough money. If only I could get that many pills. If only . . ." is the anthem of the addict. You keep going after that first high, but you can't ever find it. So you keep hunting and lying to get it. Nothing is as important as the momentary oblivion of getting high. Every detail at the altar of my addiction had been meticulously planned out and tested: how to get the most bang for my buck and how to get the best high from the drugs, chewing up the pills on an empty stomach. Man, I'd chewed up a lot of pills, which meant a lot of empty stomachs. I had lost so much weight. As though on cue, my stomach grumbled with hunger.

The sun was rising in the east, the purple and orange hue of a new day. There was no way I was going to make it home before my wife got up. Boy, was I in for it. She was going to see right through me. There was going to be shouting this morning. I started thinking up a story. My stories kept getting more and more ridiculous. But I didn't care. Everything came in second to the one and only true love of my life: getting high.

The little relief from my nap beside the road was already wearing off. I wouldn't have much time before I would have to start this entire process all over again. This is how it was every day. Never a break. Something had to give. And since addiction doesn't give to anyone, it would be me who gave everything. This week I would test out my new idea. I would try out my new con.

"Darvocet—unbelievable. I hate Darvocet."

Chapter 3

The Con

I showed up at the pharmacy early because I had nothing else to do. Early because it was all I could think about. Early because I had nowhere else to go. People went in and out of the pharmacy. Just a normal, ordinary day for most people. It was disturbing to think that this was an ordinary day for me.

Calling in my own prescriptions had become an easy way for me to acquire my drug of choice. Unfortunately for me, I was good at it. The first time I attempted it, I succeeded. It would've been better for me if I hadn't because, ever since, I was hooked. All the times I had gone to the doctor and faked a back injury, the absence of my tooth still fresh in my mind—this was so much easier. Hearing so many prescriptions called in was finally paying off. I wished I had tried this much sooner.

I remember the first time I tried it. Driving away, I felt incredibly exhilarated—high before I even took the drug. Soon, I was as helplessly addicted to the adrenaline rush of getting the drugs as the opiate rush of using them.

However, increased availability leads to increased usability. I was using way too much. I knew it. But I couldn't stop it.

I gave myself an internal pep talk, making sure to rehearse what I was supposed to say.

Darkness Will Not Overcome

This pharmacy was like all the others. I looked around as nonchalantly as possible, trying to pick up any hint that something was amiss. I felt stares that weren't there.

"I have a prescription to pick up," I said to the woman at the window.

"What's the name?" she responded. I evaluated and inspected every bit of inflection, tone, and mannerism for the slightest hint of suspicion.

What name had I given this time? I had used so many different ones over the past couple of years. The pharmacy assistant's eyes seemed to burn holes into my soul. I felt filleted, laid open, exposed.

"David Johnson," I told her.

"One moment," she said as she went to the computer.

I had stopped using my own name, for obvious reasons. If they looked up my information, became suspicious, they had everything: address, name, phone number. Next thing I would know would be the sheriff banging down my door. So I started using a different identity every time. This posed its own set of problems. Like if they asked for identification. This had happened several times, to which I had to respond with an innocent, "I forgot my ID in the car," only to leave the store, jump in my car, and take off.

The seconds crept by with agonizing slowness as the lady typed away on the computer.

"Have you ever had a prescription filled here?"

"I don't think so," I said with an air of innocence as if to say, "I never get prescriptions filled." This was the second prescription today.

"I'm going to need some information." She asked me for my address, date of birth, allergies.

Would this be the time I would get caught? Eventually, you give in to the reality that you will get caught. It isn't *if*, but *when*. The sad thing was that I had reached a point where I didn't care.

The Con

You go from thinking days ahead to only highs ahead. If I can just get that next hit, I'll worry about getting caught—and quitting—later. It's all about the next high. Everything else is fuzzy; everything else, forgotten.

The lady left the computer to go around the corner. What was the verdict? Would she come around the corner with the pharmacist, threatening arrest—or with a bottle of pills?

Beads of sweat started appearing on my brow. It felt like my soul was sweating, like every pore on my body was mouthing the word *guilty*. One of the hardest things about this part of the con is acting like you don't care when it is the only thing you really care about—an intentional, organized nonchalance—when inside you feel anything but nonchalant.

She came back around the corner.

"Mr. Johnson, we have your prescription ready." She used an ordinary tone of voice, completely unaware of the drama I had just played in my mind.

"Do you need to ask the pharmacist any questions about the medication?" she asked.

"I don't believe so."

The irony is when the pharmacist comes and gives me the directions the doctor had given him to give me, which was really me giving them to me—all a part of the con. What made the trick was the details. The more details, the more real it seems.

I paid for the prescription and told them thank you. Elated, I walked out of the store. With a determined nonchalance, I strolled through the parking lot, ready for the SWAT team to drop through the ceiling, ready for the sheriff to pull up in front of the store, ready for something to catch me in the act. But nothing came.

The vicious cycle of chemical dependency. We use drugs to escape reality, the reality of pain or boredom. The problem is you don't just escape what you want. You escape the things you don't want, too, such as God, family, job, and responsibility. Before long, the escape starts accumulating a list of consequences. The job losses. The marital problems. The child endangerment. Being surrounded by the consequences of "the escape"—overwhelmed by guilt, shame, and regret—creates even more desire to escape. Thus, your solution and your problem are the same thing. The "vicious cycle" continues. Reality is the problem—you are the problem. Unfortunately, no matter what you do, you still remain unchanged. I would be done with this bottle of pills by this time tomorrow. I would be more raw, empty, and broken on the other side of this high than I was now. I knew this, but I couldn't stop. No matter what I did, I still remained unchanged. I was left to linger in my own prison for a while longer, to continue in the downward spiral into oblivion.

I pulled out of the parking lot, popped ten pills in my mouth, and started chewing them up. The chalky bitterness had become sweet to me. It was bitter in the mouth but sweet to my mind because I knew the numbing was coming.

Chapter 4

A Visit to Church

One day, I had unavoidably been forced to go to church, a place I avoided as much possible. But that day, I showed up late and left early. My wife gave me sideways glances throughout the service, no doubt hoping inside that I might become born again, that a line from the sermon, a note from a hymn, or a word from a prayer might make it through to me. But too often these days, her hope was dashed by reality. It isn't just the addict who lives an up-and-down, high-and-low life. The ones who love the addict live it too. Just when they start hoping against hope that the addict is changing—or maybe, just maybe, getting a little better—something happens to dash that hope against the cliff of reality.

The pastor's appeal felt eternal. It felt like a thousand eyes from heaven and earth were watching me like I was a spectacle, some kind of exhibition. It felt like the pastor was talking to me, as though he were praying with one eye open—pointed right at me. I couldn't take it anymore, so I quietly stepped out of the pew and headed toward the back door. I definitely didn't want to talk to anyone. I came to church. I showed up. That should be enough. That should satisfy my wife for at least a little while.

As I exited the church and made my way through the parking

lot to my car, I heard someone behind me call out my name. It was my high school teacher, Mr. Cornell. I was never any good at chemistry, math, or science—the classes he taught. But there he was, chasing me down. He was one of those teachers who saw something in his students that they themselves could not see.

"Hey, Richie, you got a second?"

No, I didn't have a second. No, I didn't want to talk. I had no desire whatsoever to hear the little pep talk, the inspirational tidbit, I was getting ready to endure.

"OK." My lack of interest was apparent. He was wearing one of the sports coats he had made. Was there nothing this guy could not do?

"I am not sure what's going on right now, Richie, but God impressed me to say something to you," he said as I tried to produce the closest thing to an authentic smile that I could.

"Great," an obvious lie that Cornell saw through.

"Richie, I know you're not doing well. I can tell. I just wanted you to know I've been praying for you. I would like to have a quick prayer with you right now. Would that be OK?" he asked, not caring what my answer to that question was.

"I really have to go—"

"It will be quick," he said, putting his arm around my shoulder and praying before I had a chance to object.

I don't remember much about the prayer. I had other things on my mind. But for a moment, my mind went to the scene in the Bible, at the Last Supper, when Jesus says, "Simon, Simon, behold, Satan demanded to have you, that he might sift you like wheat, but I have prayed for you that your faith may not fail. And when you have turned again, strengthen your brothers" (Luke 22:31, 32). Jesus prayed for Peter even though He knew he was going to deny Him. Jesus chose Judas to be a disciple even though He knew he was going to betray Him. This must have been what it felt like for Judas, standing in a circle, holding hands with the other disciples, as Jesus prayed for what seemed

A Visit to Church

like an eternity, knowing full well what he was on his way to do, knowing full well he had no intention of changing his mind. Maybe this is what the Bible meant when it said, "Then Satan entered into Judas called Iscariot, who was of the number of the twelve" (Luke 22:3). Like me, I wonder whether Judas couldn't stop even if he wanted to. Maybe he loved the sound of silver clinking in his pocket like I loved the sound of pills rattling in mine. Jesus cared more for Peter, Judas, and all the disciples than they cared for themselves. I saw that same care become flesh and blood as Mr. Cornell prayed with me that day. He cared more than I cared. "But I have prayed for you that your faith may not fail. And when you have turned again, strengthen your brothers."

He said, "Amen," and I quickly said, "Bye."

I remember pulling out of the church parking lot and seeing Mr. Cornell in my rearview mirror watching me pull away. He watched with sad eyes and slumped shoulders. It was a pitiful expression of loss, one of the many reasons I avoided church. I had more important things to do. There wasn't room in my life for anything other than getting high.

Chapter 5

Trouble at Kmart

A tinge of nostalgia hit me as I walked into the Kmart. The fluorescent lights and plastic smells took me back to a time when, as a child, I would make a beeline for the toy section. This time I was making a beeline for the pharmacy.

I had called in the prescription earlier. I had stopped in about thirty minutes before, only to be told it wasn't ready and to check back in about thirty minutes. I sat in my car, watching the clock on my dash for every single minute. The moment thirty minutes were up, I was up and out of my car.

I should've seen the signs. Looking back, they were obvious: the overly happy disposition of the pharmacist, the whispers and glances behind the desk, the police cars sitting randomly in the parking lot. The tunnel vision had blinded me—and not for last time. Something wasn't right. Somehow, deep down, I knew it as I made my way back through the store, past the toy section, to the pharmacy.

"Is my prescription finished now?" I asked the pharmacy tech who had told me to come back.

"We almost have it done," he said. Immediately I realized they were on to me.

"Thanks." I turned as calmly as I could and started heading toward the entrance.

Trouble at Kmart

Before I was close enough for the automated sliding doors to sense my presence and open, three police cars, with lights on—the ones I had seen "randomly" scattered in the parking lot—pulled up in front of the door. No point in running. The policemen were out of their cars before I could turn around.

"Sir, stay where you are. Are you Richard Halversen?" they asked as they quickly approached me. I couldn't say anything. I was speechless.

"Turn around."

They handcuffed me and then escorted me back in the direction I came, toward the pharmacy. Mothers pulled their children close. Fathers looked at me like I was the problem with the world. Children looked at me like I was the scariest thing they'd ever laid eyes on. It felt like every person in the world was in that Kmart—watching me, gawking at me—as the police took me to the pharmacy. It's bad enough to be arrested, but in Kmart, it felt worse. This was bad.

"Is this him?" they asked the pharmacist and tech behind the counter.

"Yes," came the reply. Expressions behind the counter always fall into two categories. Either an expression of pity or an expression of gleeful satisfaction—one more "junkie" off the streets.

The police turned me around and walked me back to the front of Kmart where their cars were parked.

"Watch your head," the one leading me said as he pushed my head down and put me in the back of his police car. He went up to the other policemen and said something. I couldn't tell what they said, but I did hear their laughter, and when he turned around, he was smiling. He got in the car, turned off his lights, and looked at me through the rearview mirror. He radioed dispatch as he pulled out of the Kmart parking lot. Suddenly, the reality of my situation came crashing in.

"What happens now?" I asked, afraid of what I was about to hear.

"We'll take you downtown and process you."

"What does that mean?"

"It means we will fingerprint you. Write up a report. Place you in a holding cell until the judge sees you. Then the judge will set the bail amount," he said, unmoved. This was just a normal day for him.

"When does that happen?" I asked.

"When does what happen?"

"How long does it take for the judge to set bail?"

"It depends. But usually within a few hours."

The rest of the drive to the Davidson County processing station in Nashville was relatively quiet. As we got close to the station, the police officer, sensing my apprehension, gave me a little pep talk.

"You need to get some help," he said.

"Yes, you're right," I said, hoping that maybe my malleable attitude would earn me points with the police officer, as if he would pull over and open my door and say, "Well, it sounds like you've learned your lesson. Go on, get out of here, young man."

"You don't have to live this way. I've seen so many people end up in a bad place from this. At best, you end up in prison; at worst, you end up dead. It is no way to live. Do you have any kids?"

"Two."

"Do it for their sake, man. They need their dad."

"Yeah."

This officer was relatively nice. Over the coming months and years, I would interact with many who were not. Some police took their bad days out on their prisoners. They treated you like you were an animal. Maybe that was because you start looking and acting more like an animal than a human being. However, like this officer, some saw the person underneath the disease. They saw their career as their calling. They didn't just want to arrest people; they wanted help keep people from having to be arrested. This police officer, Officer James, was like that. Instead of looking at me like I was a worthless piece of scrap, he recognized the humanity deep down in me.

We pulled up to a garage. He pushed the intercom. Seconds later, the door started rising. As the door closed behind us, it felt like a part of my life had been closed off too. I had just entered a new low in living. I had become one of "those people" whom I had sworn I would never become.

Officer James helped me out of the police car. It is hard to get up or sit down when your hands are cuffed behind your back. He unlocked the handcuffs and removed them. They were no longer necessary. I was secured, locked up.

A guard came up to Officer James. He handed him a clipboard. Officer James signed it. Then the guard took me by the arm and led me up the stairs.

"Good luck," Officer James said as he watched me ascend the stairway. Judgment day had arrived. All of my illegal activity had seemed to be building up to this moment.

"Thanks." I didn't need luck. I needed help—desperate help.

I was led into a room where I was photographed and fingerprinted. There was a first time for everything. They had me wash my hands and then gave me some Corn Huskers Lotion. Apparently, it helps the fingerprinting process. The smell of the lotion filled my nostrils like sweet-smelling corruption. I will never forget that smell. This memory will forever be associated with my demise, this cold, fluorescent room where I felt so completely empty and broken.

They took me from there to see the judge. I went into a small room. The judge was sitting behind a thick pane of glass. He read me the charges.

"Mr. Halversen, you are charged with prescription fraud. It is a class D felony that can carry two to twelve years in state prison, depending upon your criminal history. Do you understand?"

"Yes." Two to twelve years? Unease turned into panic. *It's over.*

Darkness Will Not Overcome

I'm forever ruined. They are going to lock me up and throw away the key.

"You have no previous criminal record, so you should qualify for pretrial diversion, which will allow you to be released without bail being set. Here is your court date. Be there, Mr. Halversen." Instant relief washed over me, causing me to briefly forget that I had started withdrawing. He looked past me to the guard standing behind me. The guard took me by the arm and led me away.

The guard guided me down a hallway to a large, steel door. He motioned to another guard behind glass at the end of the hall. The door buzzed and opened. There were about twenty people in the room, all recent arrests. Everyone was sitting on the metal benches that lined the inside of the room, with the exception of a homeless man who lay on the floor. He had a small puddle near his groin. Based on the smell that smacked me, there was no doubt. It was urine.

"Sit down. They'll call you when they're ready for you," the guard said as I tried to avoid the puddle of urine on my way to the only small, vacant seat in the room.

"What about my phone call?" My only reference of jail up to this point was the movies.

"They're right there on the wall," he replied.

Four phones lined one side of the room. All the phones were taken except for one; the one not taken was right between two really big, really ugly, rough-looking dudes. I went in for the phone anyway. Surely they wouldn't hurt me in here. There were too many witnesses. I tried to fake strength with my stride. I was forty pounds underweight, literally a walking stick. Who was I kidding?

"Excuse me," I said, pointing to the unused telephone. He didn't move or even look in my direction. With great fear and trepidation, I reached out and grabbed the phone, sitting down in the tiny space on the bench. There was only enough room for me to halfway sit in the space. That was OK. I wasn't going to complain.

I picked up the phone. The only way to make calls was collect, and of course, when you call collect, it announces, "Richie Halversen (a recording of your stated name) is calling you collect from the Davidson County jail. Will you accept?" Who in the world could I call that would not freak out at that message? My wife? Definitely not. My parents? No way. My in-laws? Ludicrous. And then it hit me—my sister April. That's who I'd call.

I have two sisters, Jennifer and April. Jennifer, being the typical elder sister, was like Mom #2; at least, she assumed that role whether she was given it or not. In fact, sometimes, Mom #2 knew—or thought she knew—better than Mom #1. April and I were only fourteen months apart and pretty close, so at times we would have to join forces to take on the big, bad older sister: Jennifer.

When I was about seven years old, I had a hard time sleeping in my room alone. I had seen something scary on the television, and it had damaged my ability to sleep alone in my room. So I would sneak into my sister's room.

April would smuggle me into her covers, covering me up so that Jennifer wouldn't find me. Jennifer felt it was her responsibility to nip that bad habit in the bud. If she roused from her sleep and found me in her room, she took it upon herself to teach me a lesson and drag me back to my room.

"Sorry, Richie, it is for your own good," she would say as she led me back to my bed. I can honestly say she did mean it for my own good, and I loved both my sisters. However, if Jennifer found out I was doing something wrong, she felt obligated to tell my parents. Once, I had been caught smoking in the bathroom in high school. I then made a fake phone call to my parents in front of my dean. That performance could've won an Oscar. I thought I had gotten away with it. However, your sins will eventually find you out. Jennifer's friend mentioned it to Jennifer, and the rest was history. Jennifer told my parents, and I was grounded for a month. April, on the other hand, knew how to keep a secret. We had each other's backs.

I picked up the phone and dialed my sister. Thank God, she picked up.

"Hey, Richie, what's up?" she asked.

"Hey, April. Well, it's kinda crazy, but I was arrested for driving with a suspended license."

"What!" she exclaimed.

"Yeah, can you do me a favor? Would you please come down to Nashville and pick me up?"

"OK, yeah," she said.

"Thanks, April." I tried to hide the desperation in my voice. "I really appreciate it."

I hung up the phone, feeling sicker with each minute that passed. Jail is a pretty miserable place. It's even worse when you're dope-sick.

It was dinnertime. The door opened, and a guard pushed in a cart loaded with trays of food. Dinner was made up of ham, cornbread, and a pile of what looked like spinach. It was actually collard greens, a southern favorite that I had never eaten up to this point. I still couldn't eat collard greens; my stomach turned just thinking about it. The only thing my body wanted was to get high. Until I did, it was going to reject everything else I tried to give it.

The guard handed me a tray.

"No, thanks," I said.

The words were hardly out of my mouth when the big guy to my left, the one who was three times my size, leaned over to me and said, "You better get that tray, boy."

Without hesitation, I said, "On second thought, I think I will take it."

The guard handed me the tray, and my big neighbor immediately—without pause or permission—took it out of my hand. We didn't say another word to each other. He ate his second tray of food with the same authority as his first. How could these people eat in here? The odor of urine and body odor was strong.

A few hours went by, and finally, the door opened again, and a guard called my name.

"That's me," I almost shouted as I jumped up.

"Follow me," he said. I followed the guard through a couple of sliding doors and had a seat in front of a glass partition. Behind the glass partition, another guard was sitting.

"Your sister is here to pick you up." Overwhelming relief flooded my mind.

"You need to fill out these forms. Here is your court date. Don't miss it!" the guard said expressionlessly.

"Yes, ma'am." I finished filling out the papers in a few minutes. I gave them back to her, and she pushed a button that buzzed a door open beside the glass.

I walked out into another hallway and then out another door into a warm Nashville summer night. My sister was outside the car; her husband, Ben, sitting behind the wheel. She walked up to me with a look of disappointment and concern and hugged me. It was a look April has given me a lot in the past. Much more in recent years. The guards had told them why I was arrested when they came to pick me up. So much for my charade. So much for the elaborate lie I had spent so much time crafting.

My sister April is the quiet one. She didn't speak for a few minutes. Nervous as to how to approach me, I'm sure. Ben focused on driving.

"Richie, what's going on?"

"Nothing. It was stupid. I don't know why I did it. I was just messing around." I kept downplaying it as though I lifted a pack of gum from a convenience store. She didn't immediately respond with words, but her tears spoke volumes in their rivulets and streams.

"Richie, this is serious."

"I know."

"They're charging you with a felony. They said you need to make sure you get a good attorney. This is a big deal," she said as she kept shaking her head.

"I don't know what I was thinking. But I promise I'll never do it again. I promise." I made the promise knowing that I was going to break it. "Did you tell Mom?"

"Of course I told Mom," she responded. Her sadness quickly turned to anger. "Mom thinks you need to come home with us, and then we'll figure out what we're going to do."

"Well, first I need to get my car," I said, the familiar panic returning. Whenever something came between me and getting high, the panic, the desperation, the endorphins would kick in. I would do anything. I would lie to anyone. No theft was off-limits. It didn't matter if it was family or the old lady down the street. Nothing except for using was sacred to me anymore.

"Why don't you leave the car tonight, and we will pick it up tomorrow?" Ben suggested. His first words. He was in that awkward place in-laws sometimes have to be when the veil is pulled back and realization kicks in. My family is broken; their family is broken. Their problems suddenly become your problems. Their baggage suddenly becomes your baggage.

"No, I have got to get my car," I almost shouted. I had to get my car because I had to get high. They saw it even though I didn't say it. "I need to be able to have my car. I have things I have to do tomorrow." Like, get high.

"We don't think that's a good idea," April joined in.

"I don't care if you think it's a good idea or not." Panic turned to frustration, and then anger. "If you don't take me to my car, I'm going to jump out of this moving car and walk there myself." My sister's tears began falling again.

"Just take him to his car, Ben," she said. Ben resigned with a sigh and took the exit to the Kmart where my car was still parked.

Trouble at Kmart

"Don't worry about me. I'll come straight to the house," I said, trying to recover from my outburst. He pulled into the parking lot. My car sat there—alone, vacant, like something forgotten—surrounded by empty spaces, like my life. The car stopped. I jumped out. "I'll see you in a few minutes." My brother-in-law and my sister did not look convinced. I got my keys, opened my car, and started it up. They stayed beside me for a moment before they began to leave. I started behind them, allowing the distance to increase. As they got on the ramp to head back up the interstate, after they couldn't turn around, I drove straight instead of turning and headed for the on-ramp heading in the opposite direction. Back into the city. Back into my insanity. I'd eventually make it to their house. I had nowhere else to go. My wife was definitely not going to let me come back home. But first, I had to get high. I had to get enough to last me into tomorrow. Just some to take the pain away.

I went right back to the same thing I had just gotten arrested for. I didn't even hesitate. It was as though this day hadn't just happened. I couldn't stop. I was trapped. It didn't matter how hard I tried; I couldn't stop myself.

Chapter 6

Twin Falls

Several months after that first arrest, I was arrested again, in the small town of Lafayette, Tennessee. Apparently, it was big news for the small town because it made the front cover of their small newspaper. "Man arrested for calling in his own prescriptions," it read.

"Is that you?" one of my fellow inmates asked.

"Unfortunately, yes," I replied, looking at my name on the printed page.

My parents were in town. I tried to get them to bail me out, but instead of coming to get me, they left me a note.

"Richie, we're sick. We cannot do this anymore. Your father and I don't have the money. We love you, but we're not bailing you out." A Bible verse was written at the bottom. "But I will call on God, and the Lord will rescue me. Psalm 55:16" (NLT).

She signed it, "We love you, Mom & Dad."

Addiction is a disease that affects not only the addict but also everyone who loves the addict—the spouse, the parents, the children, the friends. Addicts end up hurting most the ones who love the addict the most. It creeps into their minds: constant worry, constant suspicion, paranoia, sleepless nights anticipating a phone call notifying them that the addict has been arrested—or,

TWIN FALLS

worse, killed. Just when they think the addict is getting better, the addict sinks to a whole new low, hitting a bottom that goes deeper and deeper. Hope continues to erode until there's not much left to hold on to. They keep trying different things to get through to the addict, but nothing seems to get through.

In one of these attempts to get through to me, after a week in jail, my parents flew me out to where my dad was doing a three-week revival series in Twin Falls, Idaho. I had worn out my welcome at home and so decided to take them up on the offer. Traveling is not usually something an addict wants to do. Too many variables, of which the main one is, where will I get drugs? So I made sure to stock up as much as I could before I went.

My parents were bringing me out to get a closer look at me. They wanted to see whether I was really clean. (I wasn't.) Upon release, I went straight back to using.

The plane touched down in Boise, Idaho, where they were picking me up. It was a cold day in March.

My parents waited for me at the baggage claim. All I had was a backpack, although I had a whole lot more (invisible) baggage than that.

When my parents saw me, they were taken back. Once the nightmare is visible and you see it with your own eyes, reality comes crashing in. I had lost so much weight in the short time since we were last together. I just wanted to get high. I ate only because I had to.

My mother hugged me. I felt the heartbreak in the hug, a palpable squeeze of desperation, as though she was trying to keep me from falling apart. I could see the horror in my dad's eyes, although he tried to seem optimistic. Your children are always your children. Regardless of what they do, the crimes they commit—even if they do the unthinkable—they are still your children. The mind always goes back to better times when they were young. It's easy to think back to better times than to face the reality of the present. When everyone else saw a junkie, my mom and dad saw their son—their only son. I was always a momma's boy. I was her little admirer. "No one is as pretty as you, Mom," I had often said. I hated being away from home growing up. I even had separation anxiety when going away to school for a few hours. For me, as a kid, there was nothing like the reassuring feeling of being at home and together. But I had become something else entirely. There was only a small remnant of that small boy left, a forgotten voice in a deep, dark, empty space.

I threw my backpack in the back seat and got in the passenger side for the two-hour drive to Twin Falls. We didn't say much in the beginning. No one wanted to deal with the obvious. No one wanted to talk about the elephant in the room, at least not yet. Too soon in the trip to put a damper on things.

"Are you hungry?"

"Sure, I can eat something."

"Where do you want to eat?" my father asked.

"Anywhere is fine."

Before long, my mom couldn't contain herself. "Richie, how have you been doing?"

"I'm good." Everyone could see I was not good. I was anything but good.

"I've been doing some reading." Here it came. My mom began unloading everything she had learned about drug addiction over the past couple of years. It came from her in steady streams of breath and sound. If you followed her words, you could trace them through her mouth, down her throat, and back to her heart. She was trying to eradicate the disease that was destroying me with all she had read. She wanted to tip the balances more in my favor, as though René Descartes were right when he said, "I think; therefore, I am." No. More like, "I do; therefore, I am." We are creatures of habit. If just knowing something made you something, the world would be a far better place. I had been trying to think my way out of this prison for years now. But what you discover in addiction is that the mind can know it is destroying itself and still not be able to stop it. There was more disease left than me.

My mom continued sharing her research with me as we stopped to get something to eat. I kept nodding. I needed to be agreeable right now. I had to instill confidence and trust because I would need to find a way to sneak out and get away from my parents tomorrow. My drug supply was quickly diminishing.

I think my mom did not eat a single bite of her food, and what she ate, I doubt she enjoyed. I was not the only one whose diet had suffered lately. We drove for another hour before we arrived at my parents' fifth-wheel trailer, their accommodations for the duration of their three-week-long revival event. Two inches of snow covered the ground. The high temperature that day was ten degrees Fahrenheit. I grabbed my bag and went in.

"Make yourself at home," my mom said. As I looked around the small trailer, I thought, *This is going to be interesting.*

"Thanks. I think I'm going to lie down for a few minutes, if that's OK." I lay down on the couch.

Almost every day while staying in Twin Falls, I had to come up with an outlandish reason why I needed to go into town, go to the library, or be alone. I had them drop me off at the library or a store, or I just left and then hitchhiked into town. It was still early enough in my destruction that I could still convince my parents, and others, I was not doing anything wrong. But they were not really convinced. Denial just seems easier than the truth.

Every evening I went with them to a meeting, so I only had a couple of hours mid-morning to mid-afternoon when I could escape and fake my way into getting high.

Twin Falls wasn't a large city—a population of only about 50,000 people. I don't remember much about it—one of the unfortunate byproducts of addiction. Memory is hazy, swallowed whole by the all-consuming desire and need for more. The waterfall was really the only thing that made any lasting impression.

Darkness Will Not Overcome

The falls for which the city had been named, I suppose. The flowing water—unstoppable, voluminous, and white—was like liquid clouds flowing over rocks and jagged pieces. The water couldn't stop even if it wanted to. My life had become like that waterfall, forced over the side, pushed into cracks, shoved over cliffs, reaching one level only to realize there was another one left to go down. No matter how painful it was, I kept going. I couldn't stop. Life had become comfortable in my brokenness.

Today, after the waterfall, my parents dropped me off at the library. Earlier that week, I had called in a prescription and gotten away with it.

"Hello, this is Doctor _____. I have a patient on vacation—" Ridiculous. Who goes on vacation to Twin Falls, Idaho, in the middle of the winter? But the prescription went through, no problem. If there was any suspicion, it wasn't enough to convince the pharmacist to call the police.

But today I wasn't so lucky. I called up a pharmacy, and just a few seconds into my canned con, the pharmacist interrupted me.

"I know you are not a doctor," he said matter-of-factly. "I called the doctor's office to verify, and they told me you've been using their identity for a while to call in prescriptions. I have called all the pharmacists in the area and flagged you. You're not going to be able to get a prescription filled within a hundred miles. If you try to pick up a prescription, you will be arrested." My gut wrenched. Panic set in as I quickly hung up the pay phone. But out of desperation, I went ahead and called in another prescription to see if maybe he was bluffing.

I left the pay phone and started walking in the direction the store was in. It was a mile from where I was. I zipped up my jacket to walk in the cold winter air.

When I came to the street the pharmacy was on, everything looked normal. Nothing out of the ordinary. I kept walking a little farther up, completely taking in the area, looking for anything that looked suspicious. I had learned from my Kmart episode to scope out the place thoroughly. As I approached the far side of the store—just when I thought everything was good—I walked down a side street to get a glimpse of the back of the store, and my suspicions were confirmed. Four police cars were already parked in the back. Panic grabbed me. Adrenaline pulsated through me. Immediately, I locked my head and my line of sight straight ahead, watching the police cars in my periphery. They were waiting for me. The pharmacist hadn't been bluffing; deep down, I had known he wasn't.

I picked up my stride, moving as quickly as I could without bringing attention to myself. I felt like any minute the sirens would go off and the blue lights would come on. Fortunately for me, they didn't. I kept walking, took the next side street I came to, and ran around the block. What was I going to do? Now that I knew all the pharmacies in the area were notified about me, what now? A hundred-mile radius? What in the world was I going to do? Desperate times called for desperate measures. Fortunately—or unfortunately—for me, desperate measures had become my specialty.

Never during this time did I ever think of just buying them off the street. For some reason, that was a line I had determined not to cross, a ridiculous standard considering that what I was doing was a greater offense than buying them off the street. There were other reasons too. The most practical reason was that buying off the street required more money, and more money required more manipulating, lying, and work.

Several years before this, while visiting my parents, my family and I had gone to Sun Valley, Idaho, a ski resort. I knew we were not very far from there. I called my mom from the first pay phone I came to. I told her I had finished at the library, was out walking, that I had lost track of time, and asked whether she would pick me up. She did.

When I got into the car, knowing we still had a few hours until we had to be to my dad's meeting that night, I came up with a ridiculous story of why I needed to go to Ketchum, Idaho,

Darkness Will Not Overcome

a small town near Sun Valley. Ketchum was eighty miles away. Fortunately—or unfortunately—for me, I talked my mother into it. She was desperate to believe, and to experience, the stuff of real relationships. This desperation often finds some respite in denial. You want so badly to believe things are not as bad as they seem. You exaggerate the good times and try to forget the bad ones. For me, the con worked. We got to Ketchum, and I found a small pharmacy. I called in a prescription. I was able to get away from my mom by slipping out of a store she thought I was in and picking up my prescription. Earlier that day, I had stolen one of her credit cards. Fortunately, or unfortunately, for me, the pharmacist didn't quite contact all the pharmacies within a one-hundred-mile radius. Maybe he didn't think I would take him up on his offer. I'm sure, over time, he would come to discover that addicts, as crazy and as desperate as they may be, are very predictable. They can't help but be predictable. Where there is a will, there is a way.

On the drive back to Twin Falls, my mom drove quietly, suspicious of my twenty-minute disappearing act. I tried to alleviate her doubt. I tried to change the subject. My mood had suddenly improved as I felt for the pills in my pocket. I had stuffed toilet paper into the bottle to eliminate the rattling of pills. My paranoid obsession with "how" I carried my pills would get weirder and weirder. I had contingency plans for my contingency plans. Paranoia had taken hold, and I overly thought through every scenario. What if they searched my car? What if they searched my body? What if my wife checked my pants? Addiction becomes a constant state of "what ifs" with no easy answers.

The feeling of the weight in my pocket reassured me, *Everything's going to be all right, at least for the next few hours.* The drugs had become an obsession that caused new obsessions, a habit that caused new habits.

Over the past few years, I was not the only one who had developed a habit. Addiction can go one of two ways. You can throw in the towel and indulge it, which will kill you—spiritually, emotionally, and eventually, physically—but if you resist it, you'll have to hold on to something bigger and more powerful than yourself. You cannot resist it in your own power. Sure, you may resist the drugs, but the addiction will manifest in something else. My mom resisted the temptation to give in to the seeming hopelessness of my addiction. And the only way she found to fight my demise was through prayer.

My parents always had the habit of praying. But when the life of someone you love is on the line, it thrusts you into a deeper understanding of prayer. There is nothing like pain and desperation to tear away the veneer of theatrical religion. It often isn't until you reach the end of your rope that you reach out and take the hand of God. The disease of addiction is great at creating helpless situations. The addict is helplessly caught up in the obsession and compulsion of using drugs. The family and friends of the addict are helpless to change them. Addiction thrives in helpless situations. But you know what? So does God! So my addiction took my mother's prayer life to a whole new level. There was at least one good that came out of all this bad.

She wrote all of her prayers in journals. She often tells us, her three children, that we will inherit those prayer journals when she dies. My sisters, who rarely got into anything that could even be considered trouble, will inherit volumes of my mom's prayers. I will inherit an entire library, volumes of the desperate cry of a mother whose child is slowly killing himself. When everything is stripped away and you have nothing left to hold on to, that's when you discover the power of prayer.

So while I was falling further down the rabbit hole, my mom was discovering a new level of faith and trust. In the steady darkness of anguish and pain, a light was growing brighter; a Christian was becoming a daughter.

No doubt she was praying silently as we drove back to Twin Falls. With the familiar glow of the opiates entering my

Darkness Will Not Overcome

bloodstream, my mouth became an open stream of words, crashing and cascading as, I am sure, were her prayers. While I couldn't stop talking, she couldn't stop praying.

Chapter 7

Connecting Flight

I narrowly made my connecting flight. As my plane taxied to its place on the tarmac, I pulled my shirt from my chest. It pulled away slowly, clinging to my skin, wet with perspiration from my run to the airport. I had only two hours in Atlanta. I had taken my last pills earlier that morning before I left my parents in Idaho. Withdrawals had already started kicking in before touching down in Atlanta.

"Would you like something to drink?" the flight attendant asked.

"Water, please."

With each day, with each use, the highs got shorter, dosage increased, and the withdrawals were more intense.

I knew when I got home my wife would meet me with suspicion. So in order to buy some time, keeping up the illusion that I was indeed a changed man, I would need to call in a prescription during my brief, two-hour layover in Atlanta.

There was no way I would be able to get a prescription when I got home, at least not for a while. If I did, my wife would know I was still using. One more falling out could be the end of our marriage. One more bounced check, missing credit card, or a bank account balance that didn't quite add up was all it would take for my "already hanging by a thread" marriage to disintegrate into oblivion. Very few addicts make it out of addiction alive. Even fewer marriages make it. Trust is the cornerstone of any relationship. An addict cannot be trusted. Even the addict cannot trust the addict. The relationships that matter most become the stage of some of the greatest untruths and manipulations.

I had only two hours to make it happen. Two hours from touchdown to takeoff. So as soon as we landed, I had a plan formulated. I ran to the nearest pay phone, found a phone book, and looked up the nearest pharmacy. The closest one I found was at the Peachtree Center, eight bus stops from the airport. I called in the prescription and hoped for the best.

It was a short bus ride—eight intervals of doors opening and people coming and going. My vision was shaped like the tunnels of this metro. My mother had given me twenty dollars for food to eat on the trip back. She probably thought, *Surely it's safe to give him twenty dollars. There's no way he'll be able to get any drugs with it on the flight home. Not enough time. Plus, Brittney is picking him up at the airport.* My mother would soon learn—when she got her credit card statement after my recent visit—to never underestimate the ability of the addict to innovate. Need is something that can accommodate almost anything.

I jumped out of the metro, found a directory, and located my destination. The shopping center bustled, the lunch rush in full swing. I hoped this would work to my advantage. When the pharmacy was busy, there was less time for suspicion.

I got to the pharmacy, the neon lights beckoning to me. I was greeted by the familiarity of people, retail, pills, and cosmetics. I wiped the sweat off my forehead and tucked in my shirt. After composing myself, I went right up to the pharmacist. One hour left.

"I am here to pick up a prescription."

"What's the name?" she asked. The same charade. The same desperation. I took glances at my watch, trying not to look suspicious but needing to keep an eye on my narrowing departure window.

Connecting Flight

"They're filling it now, sir. It's going to be a few more minutes." I waited for another five minutes, which felt like an eternity before the cashier returned. "Fourteen dollars and fifty-three cents, please." The sweetest sound to my ears. I handed her the twenty-dollar bill. She gave me my change. I said, "Thank you," and left the pharmacy. The second the store line was out of sight, I took off in a sprint. Only thirty minutes left.

When I got to the metro heading back to the airport, I barely made it on before the doors closed. Twenty-five minutes left.

It was an eight-minute ride back to the airport. There was a five-year-old across the aisle from me who wouldn't stop staring at me. With large smacks of his bubble gum, his eyes tracked my every move. I wondered whether he saw through the fraud that I was. Could he, on some childlike wavelength, see through my uneasy smile straight to the broken person that I was?

I got to the airport seven minutes before departure. There was no way I was ever going to make it before they closed the doors. But, by some miracle, I did. For once, the security line was short. For once, my concourse was nearest me. For once, my gate was the first one I came to. As if by some divine intervention, the way was made clear for me to make my flight. As I ran up to the gate, the agent was in the process of closing the door.

"Hold on," I yelled. "I'm on this flight. I'm coming."

"You barely made it, sir." I handed her my boarding pass. She scanned it. As I stepped on the plane, it was one minute after departure time.

The flight attendants went through the safety guidelines and the security check. The pilots told them to prepare for takeoff. As one of the attendants walked by checking seat backs and seat belts, I asked for a bottle of water.

"Of course, sir. One moment," she said as she continued along her course. The adrenaline was coursing, my addiction feeding. I was just as helplessly addicted to the process of getting the drugs as I was to using them.

Darkness Will Not Overcome

The plane cut through the dark storm clouds on its trajectory to the cruising altitude. It broke through the gray into pure light. Similarly, the drugs had started kicking in, taking me from the dark, gray storm that was my life and bursting me into the light. At least, that's the way it felt for a little bit. The storm was getting rougher, and pulling myself up above the fray, even for a second, was becoming harder and harder; the glimpses of light, shorter and shorter. I was not rising at all but barreling down toward the bottom. For a second, I remembered something I had once heard or seen on a documentary—spatial disorientation. The individual thinks they're going up when, in reality, they are going down. I was caught in my own spatial disorientation. I was falling, and everything I did to try to right myself made it worse, causing me to careen even more out of control. My perception had stopped agreeing with reality a long time ago. And very soon, my life would meet the ground in an abrupt crescendo. Who was I kidding? I no longer got high. I just got some relief for a brief amount of time, a momentary escape from all the pain I had created.

Chapter 8

Upside Down on a Bridge and in My Marriage

I was upside down on a bridge on some back road not far from my house. The seatbelt held me in place, disoriented after my car's many flips and rolls. For a second, I thought I was right-side up. I was actually upside down. It was my life.

I pushed the seatbelt buckle release and fell to the roof. Broken glass cut my forehead and hand as I desperately searched the inside of my car for my stash of drugs. People would be arriving soon, which meant the police would be arriving soon after that. I was still disoriented as I grasped around the inside of the car. I groped toward the fuse box, where I felt the familiar feel of a plastic bundle of pills. I breathed a sigh of relief, upside down, on a bridge.

I crawled out the driver-side window and almost fell into a small ravine. It was at this point that I realized how far my car had flipped and how fortunate it was that I had landed upside down on this bridge. A few feet to the left or a few feet to the right and I would have fallen into the ravine. Not much of a drop, but significant enough to probably do much worse damage. The grass glistened with the recent rain; a light mist was still falling.

Darkness Will Not Overcome

I had been driving from my home in Portland, Tennessee, back to the halfway house in Nashville where I was staying. I was in a hurry. It had just started raining. I was driving the car we had just bought, a Ford Crown Victoria, a car with rear-wheel drive that doesn't handle recently wet roads too well. Coming around a corner too fast, I started fishtailing. I lost control of the vehicle and flipped the car multiple times, eventually rolling to a stop, upside down, on a bridge.

Before I left the house, my wife and I had another fight. It seemed as though that was all we ever did anymore. She let me come home for the day to see the kids, but not long after I arrived, she started unleashing her frustration—quite understandable. She didn't really have anyone to talk to. She loved me but was ashamed of me. How do you talk to someone about someone you love but are ashamed of? Instead of sharing her pain, she did what most people do in that situation: she stuffed it down and covered it up. She smiled on cue and tried to stay off the obvious subject of "Where's Richie?" Brittney had probably been asked that a thousand times over the past few years. She was sick of the lies, the covering up for me. People eventually got the hint and stopped asking.

It wasn't always this way. We loved each other. Brittney was my lifelong crush. I was thoroughly smitten with her. She was the most beautiful girl in the world to me, not only physically attractive but also mentally attractive. Brittney is one of the smartest people I have ever met.

We started dating during the summer of 1997. I had recently graduated from high school. Barely, but I graduated. I had already gotten into the party scene a little. But little did I know that what started out as a party would end as a full-time job of pain and misery. It starts out with using the drugs, but by the time you get to the end, the drugs are using you. But before that, I had some semblance of a normal life.

Brittney and I had known each other for years. She had been

friends with my older sister, Jennifer, in high school. We had many mutual friends and often crossed paths, but we had never spent much time with each other on our own. However, the summer of 1997 was different. Many of our mutual friends did not come back to work at camp, which thrust Brittney and me together.

Late-night talks and walks through humid Tennessee evenings became more regular. I remember the evening I realized I was absolutely smitten with her. We had taken a canoe out on the lake. The moon was full in the sky, reflecting off the still water. It was hard to discern where the earth ended and the sky began. At that moment, between the laughter and the looks, I knew she liked me, and I knew I liked her.

The rest of the summer was made up of evenings like this. Trips to Nashville together, trips to Chattanooga. Our mutual friendships brought us together, but our mutual love for each other kept us together. Three months later, while I was still hoping Brittney felt as strongly about me as I did about her, she confirmed my hope and alleviated my fear and said she loved me. Little did we know that she was already pregnant with our first child, Kaleb. We would need this love for each other to keep us going. When all hope seemed lost, she clung to hope.

On January 4, 1998, Brittney and I were married in Portland, Tennessee. Marriage and parenthood required a level of responsibly and maturity I did not yet have. Still immature, still selfish, rather than rising to the occasion, I found myself drifting further into drug use. This is why I would later learn in recovery that you can't marry or move yourself out of addiction. The problem is not where you live or who you're with; the problem is with your thinking. Unless you get the help you need, marriage will only make the addiction worse, moving to a new area will only make the addiction worse, and having kids will only bring out the worst in you when in active addiction. Over the years, I have placed my wife and my two children in some dangerous places.

Darkness Will Not Overcome

Just a couple of weeks before, someone had rear-ended me. The car was totaled, hence the Crown Victoria. But before I had been able to purchase a new car, I still had to drive my old car, a Dodge Caravan, with the back crushed in and the back window gone. It really wasn't safe to drive anywhere. But when you gotta get high, you gotta get high. I told Brittney I would like to watch our one-and-a-half-year-old, Hayley. Kaleb was with his grandparents, Brittney's parents. Against her better judgment, Brittney relented and let me watch Hayley.

It was evening and it was cold, so I wrapped up Hayley with blankets and drove down to Nashville to get some drugs. The cold winter wind whipped through the van as we drove down the interstate, and I could see Hayley's eyes wide open and staring at me through the rearview mirror. It was the only part of her that was not covered with coats and blankets. I wasn't completely careless, or so I thought at the time. Fortunately for Hayley's sake, nothing happened to endanger her more. But it could have. For years, the guilt and shame of putting my children at risk would haunt me.

When I arrived home, my in-laws were waiting for me. I lied to them. They knew it. They had been following me. My father-in-law, Michael, tried to take Hayley from me. I threatened him. Five-year-old Kaleb did not know what to do, but he knew something wasn't quite right with his dad. Michael and Leslie left. Leslie had tears in her eyes and, no doubt, anger in her heart.

I would hear about this from my wife for the next few days, weeks, months. She was all alone. I had isolated her with my brokenness. Her life was a paradox. What does a wife do when she feels the need to defend the father of her children, her husband, her friend, and yet she has nothing defensible to go on? This is a common situation for the family and friends of addicts. You become more accustomed to chaos. Suspicion, confusion, and disappointment become a daily reality. You begin to distrust any semblance of a normal life. Thus, the abnormal becomes normal. Our relationship had become like this car wreck, broken and upside down. Both thoroughly disoriented, up became down and down became up. But at least my car landed on this bridge. It could be worse. Maybe my marriage would land on a bridge. Maybe there was still hope.

I stood staring at my car, upside down on a bridge. I could hear people from the houses nearby running up behind me.

"You OK, buddy?" someone asked.

"I think so," I replied.

"You probably flipped your car five times," someone else piped in. "You completely severed that telephone pole." I looked and saw that the majority of the telephone pole was on the ground, next to what was left of it sticking out of the ground. Everything is a blur. I don't remember anything after I started sliding.

"It's a miracle you're out walking around. You sure you're not hurt?" a strong Tennessee accent asked. I was hurt, all right. Maybe not from the car wreck, but from the wreck I called life.

"No, I'm fine. Just a little shook up," I said as I stared at my car. What was I going to do now? No car. No home. No life.

I called the halfway house I was staying at and let them know I had been in an accident. I would not be making the curfew. They told me I could stay at my house tonight. This was not going to go well with Brittney; we had just bought this car.

The police came. They took a report. I tried to act as normal as I could. They didn't suspect anything. They left. The tow truck came and went. The sun and its afterglow were completely gone now. I walked the three miles back home in the darkness of a cloudy night.

Chapter 9

Christmas Alone

Three weeks after the car accident, I had burned through almost all of the $3,000 we got for the totaled Crown Victoria. I made sure to meet the insurance agent to get the check instead of having them send it in the mail. My wife waited for that check to arrive in the mail for weeks, a check I had already gotten and mostly spent.

Now, I was borrowing my brother-in-law's car. I was living out of it. I had gotten kicked out of the halfway house where I had been living. I had been stealing checks from the halfway house manager. If I hadn't had the insurance money to pay him back, he would've had me arrested.

I started the engine briefly to warm up the car. Today was Christmas. I was alone. Garbage littered the bottom of the car; bottles of urine were stuffed under the seats. Merry Christmas.

Brittney and the kids were at her parents' house. She wanted them to have a good Christmas. I was in no condition to give them one. I had bought Kaleb and Hayley some presents: a play bow-and-arrow set for Kaleb and a new doll for Hayley. I bought them only to turn around and take them back the next day for a refund so that I could get high. My family deserved so much better than this.

Christmas Alone

Over the past year, I had continued to sink deeper. In and out of jails. In and out of treatment centers. I had four felony charges against me now, not to mention the smaller charges, such as bad checks and possession of narcotics. I would be going to prison for a long time—if I lived long enough to make it, that is. There were worse things than the penitentiary. I realized that now.

My breath fogged up the windshield as I looked out at the empty parking lot. Even if I wanted to change now, I doubted I could. I had come to accept my lost state. Surrendered to my sickness, the line between reality and lie became more blurred with each day. I was tired of fighting with Brittney. I was tired of all the lies. I was tired of the constant hustle to get high. I was tired of living like this. I was tired of people looking at me the way they did. The high was no longer enough. The drugs were no longer enough. How could the son of a preacher become this? I grew up in a good family. I grew up with all the advantages life could provide. But addiction doesn't care about any of that.

I stepped outside the car. It was late, or really early. The cold air smacked my frail body like a slap across the face. It was Christmas, and I was alone. There was no room for me in the inn, no hope for me at the end. I had given up.

The irony of addiction is that it starts out as a search for significance, enlightenment, or peace. But in the end, it takes those things from you, leaving you cold, naked, and empty. It takes everything significant from you. I started using because I thought it made me more interesting, but addiction couldn't be more boring. Day in, day out, it's the same thing. What a joke. It is reprieve that quickly turns into reprimand.

It was Christmas, and I was alone, pacing around my car, my home, the only thing I had left. I looked up at the sky, and for a brief moment, I thought of the Christ. Born on a night like this, in a feeding trough. God couldn't get anyone to share Christmas with Him except for a few shepherds and some animals. I didn't think I could get anyone to share Christmas with me. I couldn't get the eyes of the Baby Jesus out of my mind, swaddled and staring at me. I wished I could enter that room where He was born. With nothing to give as gifts except my brokenness, I would fall at His feet and give my last few Vicodin to Him. The angels weren't singing this Christmas evening. They were weeping. Another child of God had thrown his life away.

I would leave to visit my sister in two days. My vision of the Christ child would be replaced by another. My sister had just had her first child. I wished I could enjoy that more than I did. I wished that occupied more space in my mind than it did. But I couldn't think of anything but myself anymore, constantly caught up in my own misery.

A few days after I arrived, I would go to treatment one last time. I had already been to treatment four times. Four times it did not work. I had memorized the mantras. I had said the prayers. I had tasted the food with a clean conscience, and yet I kept going back. I kept going back to the emptiness. I kept going back to the predictable chaos of addiction. This would be the last time I ever went to treatment. I knew this partially because of my parents' final appeal. "Richie, this is it. We don't have any more money. We don't have any more to give. We're done watching you kill yourself." But deep down I knew that if I couldn't get clean now, I'd never be clean again. I'd used up all my bottoms. I had no place left to go. The only reason I was even going to treatment was because I had nowhere else to go.

I got back in my car and turned the engine off for a little bit. I wrapped up in my jacket and spent the rest of Christmas looking out my windshield, watching cars come and go. I was alone. I had nowhere left to go. There was no room in the inn for Jesus or for me.

Chapter 10

Gooding, Idaho

When the plane landed, the captain's voice came through the speaker, "Welcome to Boise, Idaho. It is a balmy zero degrees, with a high today of two."

Someone from the treatment center was scheduled to pick me up. I grabbed my backpack and waited in line until the plane emptied. I went straight to the bathrooms and chewed up the last few pills I had left. To most people, it would be quite a few pills. But I had to chew at least ten at a time to get high anymore. My liver had to be gone.

I left the bathroom and headed for the baggage claim area. I had no baggage to claim, but it was the place I was supposed to meet the person from the Walker Center. The Walker Center is a small treatment facility in the very small town of Gooding, Idaho. If you blinked, you would miss it. The only things that really make up the town are the treatment center and a school for the blind. What a coincidence. Blind people living next to blind people. Unlike the physically blind, addicts are blind by choice, wandering through life, loaded with denial, grasping in the dark for something that holds, but nothing holds.

The person picking me up was the maintenance man. He looked to be in his seventies. He stood at the bottom of the escalator with my name on a placard. I'm pretty sure he could've picked me out without that. I had never had someone pick me up at the airport with a placard before. I thought only important, successful people were picked up by placards. For a second, I imagined that I was a successful business tycoon. A brief smile appeared and then quickly disappeared. Who was I kidding? I was a junkie. I had not done anything of significance in my whole life. The few significant things I had—my children, my wife—I'd squandered for a pocketful of pills.

The maintenance man had a kind face.

I approached him and said, "I'm Richie."

"Hello, Richie, I am John. I am with the Walker Center, here to pick you up." His entire face lit up with a smile. I had forgotten what it was like to smile like that.

"Sounds good," I said.

"Do you have any bags?" he asked, knowing the answer.

"No, just this," I said, tapping the shoulder straps of my backpack.

"All right, I am parked just outside." I followed him. Walking into the cold air was like walking into a brick wall. "Welcome to Idaho in the winter," he said with another big smile. "Do you have a larger jacket?"

"No."

"I'm sure we have something at the center you can use while you're here," he said as he unlocked the passenger-side door to a truck and opened it for me like he was a chauffeur. I got in.

The drive to Gooding took two hours. I spent most of the time staring out the window. The high desert of southern Idaho is very different from the lush green of Tennessee. It feels like another world. The wilderness seems vast, and greater, with no thick vegetation to conceal its greatness. John tried to strike up several conversations with me as we traveled, but I was distracted. My mind kept going back to the past few days at my sister's house.

Gooding, Idaho

Recently opened presents were lying underneath the Christmas tree when I got there. My sister's house looked and smelled like Christmas. It was two days after Christmas. Both of my sisters and their husbands, my parents, and my wife and kids were there. I flew separately.

Whenever I walked into the room, everyone walked on eggshells. In their eyes was love, but also pain and distrust. The awkwardness surfaced and suffused the room with a thick atmosphere of discomfort. No one knew what to say. No one knew what to do. I didn't know what to do either. So, I just stood there.

"There is food I can heat up if you're hungry, Richie," my mother said, trying to ease the tension and pretend everything was normal.

"I'm not hungry. But thanks."

Jennifer brought her newborn to me. Sydney. She was beautiful. The first grandkid since Hayley, my daughter.

"She's beautiful," I said. It was obvious to everyone that I was unable to really appreciate my new niece. I lacked the constitution. I lacked the charisma. I was sick. Weak. Broken. I did not want to hold her long lest I break her, as I was broken. Part of me wished I could enjoy Christmas and my family like I used to, but it didn't last; I had even lost the ability to wish.

Brittney avoided me for most of the few days we were together. All the lies, manipulation, and anger had been culminating to this moment. She could barely bring herself to look at me. She had been counseled to leave, no doubt. She should have. I had not been able to love her for a long time. She had become sick from sickness. My brokenness had broken her.

A few presents sat, unopened, under the tree. One of them had my name on it. The time came when I opened it. It was a "Recovery Bible." I probably had twenty Bibles at home. But this one was different; it had been compiled with the addict in mind. I opened the Bible, and the pages landed at Psalm 143:11, 12:

Darkness Will Not Overcome

> For your name's sake, O Lord, preserve my life!
>   In your righteousness bring my soul out of trouble!
> And in your steadfast love you will cut off my enemies,
>   and you will destroy all the adversaries of my soul,
>   for I am your servant.

One line stuck with me: "In your righteousness bring my soul out of trouble." I said it under my breath as we drove through the open spaces of Idaho. *Bring my soul out of trouble.*

The rest of my three days with my family are a blur. I had moments of conversations and normalcy. But the majority was more of the same. My family didn't try to stop me this time. My mom even gave me a ride to pick up a prescription. I gave her no other choice. Either she helped me just make it to Sunday when I went to treatment, or I would end up doing something stupid and getting arrested—or worse, dying. She suffered with me because she loved me. I wonder whether that is what God is like. He suffers with us because He loves us. He puts up with us because He loves us. Apparently, He thinks the pain of not having us is greater than the pain of having us. In spite of the horrible things we do, He still believes we can become the children He made us to be. "In your righteousness bring my soul out of trouble." My family had placed their last hope in the place where I was heading now: the Walker Center. They had wrapped all of their prayers and dreams in this last, great hope.

"Here we are," John said. "The booming metropolis of Gooding, Idaho." He was joking. There was only one traffic light in the middle of town and a handful of stores and restaurants.

Suddenly, my reality came crashing in all around me. *What have I done? Why did I ever agree to come here?* I thought to myself as John pulled up to the front of what looked like a small hospital. He got out of the car and opened my door like a chauffeur.

"It was a privilege meeting you, Richie," John said. "I'm sure I will see you again while you're here." He put out his hand for me

Gooding, Idaho

to shake and looked at me with two of the kindest, most patient eyes I had ever seen.

"Thank you, John," I said while shaking his hand.

"Go right inside there," he said, pointing to the front door. "There will be someone who will check you in." He paused for a second, probably sensing what I was thinking about—making a run for it. I looked past him to the school for the blind and past it to fields of nothing. There was nowhere to run. John got in his car and drove away.

I walked to the front door. My stomach felt tight; my legs, like rubber. My body was already aching from the beginnings of withdrawal.

Someone was standing at the front door, waiting for me. The second we made eye contact, she smiled through the glass.

"Hello, you must be Richie. I am Pam." She extended her hand, and I took it, my willingness to be pleasant quickly dissipating.

"Hi."

"Come, let's get you situated and settled." She guided me to her office and invited me to sit down across the desk from her. The treatment center was a reengineered wing of a hospital. The hospital still had an emergency room, but that was about it. It certainly smelled like a hospital.

Pam already had some of my information from over the phone when my mother reserved a space for me. Insurance information and personal information were among the paperwork needing to be filled out. I'd been through this so many times before, I answered without really thinking. I was already feeling sick. The pills I took when I landed were already wearing off. My tolerance had reached the point where I needed to use every few hours, at least three times a day. And that was just to get by. If I wanted to get high, I had to take at least nine to ten Lortab 10s, the usual pills I called in. Each pill had 10 milligrams of hydrocodone (the opiate) but 500 milligrams of acetaminophen. If my math is correct, every day I was taking close to 13,500 milligrams of

Darkness Will Not Overcome

Tylenol. There is no doubt in my mind that I have suffered some liver damage. But I didn't care. I had stopped caring a long time ago. You eventually reach the point in addiction where you succumb to the idea that you're probably going to die from it. I don't know how many times I went to bed not knowing whether I was going to wake up, passing out with a prayer on my mind. "Lord, don't let me die like this. I promise, if you get me through this, I will stop." The problem was that I never stopped. How many times would God listen to me? These prayers began to feel sacrilegious to me. I prayed them with no intention to follow through on anything I prayed. It was pure superstition. Just in case there was a God, I would cry to Him. Just in case the Big Guy actually took cases like mine. I wanted to pray to Him enough to get my way but not enough for Him to mess with my using and finding ways and means to use more. I was embarrassed and ashamed of some of the prayers I had prayed. So at some point, I stopped praying. I decided it was better not to pray and draw attention to myself. Maybe I could just float below the radar. It got to the point where I almost welcomed death. *Better to get high and die than to live and not get high*, I thought.

Pam was typing away when she looked up at me and asked, "Your drug of choice was opiates, correct?"

"Yes."

"How much were you taking?" I told her, but it did not seem to faze her. She had probably heard it all. I was not that unique, as far as addicts went. Same sickness, same story.

"When was the last time you used?" *Clickety-click*, her fingers danced on the keyboard.

"Four hours or so."

"How are you feeling now?" she asked.

"I'm starting to feel pretty bad." A true addict. I had been through detoxing before. Always posturing for more drugs. Wherever you're at, you play the part. Whether on the street or in the doctor's office or in detox, I always played the part to try to get more drugs. Treatment center detox drugs vary almost as much as the drugs people are addicted to. Opiate addicts get one thing, amphetamine addicts another, benzo and alcohol something else. I'm not even sure it makes a difference. But for addicts, we'll take anything if we think it's going to help. Only in treatment centers do you have people show up thirty minutes early for when drugs are passed out. We're not on time for anything else. Graduations, marriages, our children being born, you name it; we're late to it. But med time, when coming off opiates, we're there early. We are desperate to take anything. It doesn't matter if it's Tylenol or ibuprofen. It could be vitamin C, and we'll chew it, snort it, or shoot it if we think it might get us high. Just the process of using anything, seemed to help.

"We're almost finished here, and then we'll get you in to see the nurse," she said, as though reading my mind.

Just give me something, I thought.

Pam finished my registration and then escorted me to the nurses' station. I answered a bunch of her questions, many of them the same. Before long, the questions ended, and she gave me my detox cocktail. It could be better, it could be worse, and I swallowed them.

Next, I was taken to what would be my room for the next twenty-eight days. My roommate was sitting at the small desk in our room. He looked up.

"Ron, this is your new roommate, Richie. Richie, this is Ron."

"Welcome to the best room in the house," Ron said with a hint of sarcasm. He put out his hand to shake and smiled genuinely. Ron was a sixty-year-old who looked like a seventy-five-year-old. He, like me, had been to treatment several times before. He was already a week into the program. Based on the rope holding his pants up, his attire, and the drum of tobacco sitting on his desk, he had all the appearances of being homeless.

"Richie, your first group session is in twenty minutes. Get settled in, and Ron will take you to group. It is nice to meet you," Pam said as she extended her hand to shake mine. I shook it and then set my one bag on my bed and sat down with it. That was about as much settling as I had to do.

"Where are you from?" Ron asked.

"Nashville," I replied.

"Good ole Opryhouse," he said with excitement. It's actually the Grand Ole Opry, but I didn't care enough to correct him.

"Yep, that's it," I said.

"Is that where you're from originally?" I could tell Ron was the talkative type. Hooray for me.

"Basically," I said.

He looked at my name tag. He saw my last name.

"Halversen? That sounds Norwegian."

"It is."

His eyes lit up when I confirmed his suspicions. "Nice! I knew I liked you! I'm Norwegian too. Last name is Christianson. What a coincidence, they put the two Norwegians together. Are you Lutheran?" he asked and then added, "Buddhist? Hindu? Muslim? I figured since you're Norwegian maybe you're Lutheran like me. My father was a pastor." The coincidences kept coming.

"I'm not Lutheran, but my father is a pastor too."

"Really? How about that?" he said, as giddy as a teenager who had just met his college roommate. "What denomination?" I could tell he was going to keep coming back to that.

"Seventh-day Adventist."

Ron did not give me the usual, "Oh, I see," response I usually got, or the moment of awkwardness when people say, "Aren't you the ones who do not give blood?" No. "Aren't you the ones who don't pledge allegiance?" No. "Aren't you the ones—" I've heard it all. But Ron was unfazed.

"I've known a few Seventh-day Adventists. They were pretty cool people." Ron didn't speak on stuff he didn't know. He only talked about stuff he had some experience with. Over the coming weeks, I would discover Ron had experienced quite a bit. Some good, much bad.

Gooding, Idaho

"So, what's your poison?" Ron asked. There was always that question among addicts. That's the one thing that varies among us. Everything else is basically the same. Whether an alcoholic or a junkie or a crackhead, we all fall into the same traps of desperation.

"Pills. Opiates. Painkillers."

"Ah, a pill head, eh?" Ron did not wait for me to ask. Maybe he sensed I wasn't going to. "Boring ole alcohol for me. Although I've experimented with just about everything there is to take." He talked about it like war stories or battle scars. "Ever been to treatment before?" Ron asked with a smile. He already knew the answer.

"Yeah. A few times," I said with some semblance of a grin. I was ashamed of it, but I had learned to laugh about it. As they say, if you don't laugh, you'll cry.

"Me too. This is number ten for me." A fleeting vision of me at age sixty still going to treatment centers crossed my mind. I cringed at the thought. I couldn't make it another year, let alone thirty-five. It was amazing to me that someone had been able to live even this long with it.

Ron continued to talk as my mind drifted. I just wanted to get high. I just wanted to get high, go to sleep, and never wake up. I wanted to get high one more time and then die. I was tired of the lying. I was tired of all the manipulating. I was tired of all the detoxing. I was tired of hating my life and not being able to look at the person who looked back at me in the mirror.

I was reaching the point in my withdrawal when everything started hurting. Your body reminds you of your dosage. The detox meds do hardly anything to curb the pain. The bed I was sitting on hurt. The fluorescent light in our room hurt my eyes. The sound of Ron's voice hurt. I was one large, exposed nerve, everything poking at me, pushing at me. The hunger was harassing me. Ron was still talking. I nodded my head at all the appropriate times, but I was not listening.

Darkness Will Not Overcome

Over the coming weeks, I would learn to listen more. Especially to Ron. He knew a lot. Maybe he didn't practice it all the time, but he knew it. He had a way of making the best out of every situation. He was happy to be at the treatment center. He hadn't eaten this good or slept this good for months. Ron would eventually teach me to appreciate the small things. The warm shower, the hot meal, the soft bed, a simple conversation. But that was later; at this moment, I was hurting, a raging pain that shuddered through my body.

Chapter 11

The Crucible of Withdrawal

It was almost midnight. In just a few hours, it would be New Year's Day. My clean date would be New Year's Eve. That's rare. Clean dates on New Year's Day are a dime a dozen. But New Year's Eve? That's usually the day you have your last hurrah before giving sobriety one more try.

The pain was so intense now. Down to my marrow, my body screamed and shouted, every nerve receptor holding out hands like starving children. It was a type of hunger—a dark, destroying hunger—that gnawed from the darkest part of my soul. Everything hurt.

Maybe I could sneak out and get a little something, I thought. *Maybe I could sneak out the window, go into town, and make it back before the nurse ever notices that I am gone.* The moment the thought entered my mind, I recognized its insanity. How many times had I talked myself into this before? I'd left treatment earlier, against medical advice. When the going gets tough, the tough get going, but the addicts start running. Running from the sobriety. Running from the responsibility. But all the other times, I was in Nashville—my playground. I knew that town inside and out. I could beg for money. I knew who to con. I had all kinds of people to try to manipulate. But here in Gooding, I had no one. I was in what seemed like the smallest town in Idaho. It was New Year's Eve. It was about five degrees below zero outside. My thought was ridiculousness soaked in desperation. I was so used to lying to myself, it had become hard for me to know where the lie ended and where the truth began.

Ron's loud and consistent snoring made my sleeplessness even more apparent and dreadful. I got up and took a shower. It seemed to help for a second. I put the temperature up as hot as I could take it. But it didn't last long. My skin started crawling again. Nausea, diarrhea, and body aches are just a few of the symptoms of withdrawal for the opiate addict. It may not be life-threatening, but it hurts enough to make you want to die.

Turning off the shower, I put my clothes back on. I crawled in and out of bed. I paced the bedroom. *I cannot do this. I'm not strong enough. It hurts too much. It has been a whole year since I have gone a whole day without using.* For over a year, every day, my body had grown accustomed to the synthetic help of opiates. My body had forgotten how to feel good naturally.

I walked out into the hallway. The glow from the nurses' station covered everything with a clinical grey. I heard someone faintly from within but did not see them. In the hallway, there was one pay phone—the only phone accessible to us. A small phone book was stuffed in the drawer underneath. This was my routine. Go to a pay phone. Pull out the phone book. Start calling in prescriptions. The phone book for Gooding and surrounding areas was only about a quarter-inch thick. It was a small town in the middle of nowhere. Why did I ever agree to come here? I was at least six hundred miles from anyone I even remotely knew. Where would I go? Even if I did get some drugs, where would I go? My parents had been clear; my wife had been clear—everything summed up by the last thing my wife said to me before I got on the plane: "If you don't stay clean, don't come home," she had said, the overwhelming hurt apparent in her gaze. But there was something else in that gaze too. Something I

The Crucible of Withdrawal

had not seen for quite some time. A look of hope. That maybe, just maybe, she would have her husband back. That maybe, just maybe, this would be the time everything would click. But it was such a long shot; she let it rise to the surface for only a second before stuffing it deep down below, putting that hope with all the other broken hopes from recent years. There comes a point where it hurts too much to hope anymore. I couldn't blame her. I had pushed her to this point. The constant anxiety over my getting arrested, over hiding their money from me, over the possibility of my dying. It became too much.

I opened the phone book to "ph." There were only ten pharmacies in the entire phone book, only one of which was open twenty-four hours, and it was forty-five minutes away from where I was. The nurses were laughing about something. Probably over something their young children did or said. I stared blankly at the "pharmacy page" like I had a thousand times before, thinking through the scenarios, thinking about how I could make impossibility a possibility. And that's when I heard it. That's when God spoke for what seemed like the first time in forever.

I don't know if it was really God or simply a side effect of my withdrawal. But I had withdrawn many times before and never heard anything like this. As I stood in the hallway of the Walker Center, in the small town of Gooding, Idaho, contemplating leaving treatment, I heard a voice say, "Richie, if you go out that door, you will die, but if you give Me your life, I promise you, you will live again."

It was so audible, so real, that I looked around, half expecting Ron to be behind me playing some sort of sick joke. But it was only me, alone, with Someone else. Suddenly, warmth filled me. I still hurt, but I felt lighter than I had ever felt before. It was a reassuring glow that barely abated the pain of withdrawal, but it abated enough for me to think straight for just a second. I could go out that door and die—or worse, continue living the way I was—or I could stay here for a little bit longer.

Darkness Will Not Overcome

I put down the phone book and walked back to my room. Ron was still deeply asleep. I walked over to my bed, and for the first time in a long time, I got down on my knees and folded my hands, just as I had been taught as a child, the son of a preacher man. I looked over my shoulder to make sure Ron wasn't watching, or anyone else. And I prayed. I cried. I wept. The prayers poured out of my mind like the tears that were running down my face.

I was broken and, for the first time, open to something other than myself to direct my course. I finally felt as though I had hit the proverbial bottom because, for the first time, the ground underneath me felt solid enough to hold my weight.

"I am tired, God," I whispered. "I am empty. I am broken. I don't even know how to be a 'normal' person anymore. I am so incredibly alone and lost. Help me—change me! Show me how to live again." It was a short prayer but concise. It seemed perfectly sufficient for the One who was with me. He could take that small prayer and turn it into something great.

I got up slowly and crawled back into bed. Everything still hurt just as strongly as before. But there was something else with me now. For the first time in a long time, I felt something good inside of me—not the usual feeling of something missing but of something present.

I looked at the digital clock on my side table. In a few hours, I would have made it through my first day, in over a year, clean. One day that had felt like an eternity. But, as I lay there in bed, I started thinking of something other than the drugs. I started thinking about my five-year-old son's inquisitive questions. I could almost see my two-year-old daughter's sweet smile. I could almost feel my wife's touch and taste her kiss. I heard something deep within my heart, a Bible verse. I have no idea where it came from, but I heard it, as clear as crystal. "Look . . . and see; wonder and be astounded. For I am doing a work in your days that you would not believe if told" (Habakkuk 1:5).

Chapter 12

The Ropes Course

I had slept through the night for the first time since entering treatment. Two weeks. Each day was a little better than the day before. Each day, my mind got a little clearer, my thoughts a bit more rational and concise.

Food had started tasting better. Laughing became more genuine. So many things you took for granted while using start being reborn in recovery. What was only used for survival in addiction starts to be appreciated for what it truly is. Not a means to an end but a glorious end in and of itself. Food is meant not just to sustain us but to be enjoyed by us. Taste buds start exploding with flavor.

Leaving the cafeteria, I walked with a group headed toward the ropes course. The ropes course was a team-building exercise, a trust-building experiment, a series of narrow walks, steep climbs, and wiggly walks that taught us to listen to someone else for a change. For addicts, to take directions instead of constantly giving them, to let go and let someone else guide you, is very difficult.

Several of those currently at the Walker Center had been here before, and they couldn't help but let the cat out of the bag about the ropes course. Their excitement was palpable. "It's a game changer," they said. I couldn't help but think, *Apparently, it didn't change your game too much since you're here again.* I had been in treatment so many times before, I thought the same thing about myself. *How do I know I will get it this time? How do I know I will stay clean?* My thoughts rushed to these questions many times. I tried to keep busy to avoid thinking too much.

We walked out the door and assembled in front of the ropes course, a giant, wooden square raised twelve feet. One side of the square was three tight ropes—two tightropes for holding on and one for your feet. One section was just a narrow plank; another section was a series of tires. The fourth side of the square was a series of wooden steps that swung just a bit when you were on them.

We stood there, gaping at the course. As the instructors began to explain the process and go over safety protocol, the irony of a bunch of addicts listening to safety protocol brought a little smile to my face. Everyone who went on the ropes course would wear safety lines. If we fell, we would have something holding us up. I looked around at my newfound friends. Partners in my journey. The fellowship of my recovery. It felt good not to be alone anymore, not to have to be constantly looking out for myself. To be able to start looking out for someone else for a change was a breath of fresh air. It is something "normal" people do all the time. It may not seem like much, but for addicts, it's huge because it isn't something we have done in a long time. Just small efforts of looking out for someone else is massive in recovery. There was no doubt in my mind that I was still a very selfish person. Self-absorbed. But every time we were sitting in a group, listening to someone else's hardships, I felt the grip of my own insanity begin to loosen a little. It had allowed me to start breathing again. You don't realize how much energy self-obsession takes until you get a little break from it. In those moments, you realize how much you've been holding your breath. Always worrying: *What am I going to do? What am I going to get?*

The Ropes Course

What is going to happen to me? You are in charge of everything, and everything starts falling apart, and you lack the strength, wit, and power to hold it all together. What a relief to listen to and learn from someone else for a change. I had started breathing again.

I had been asked several times by fellow patients to sit in on their First Step. Basically to listen in and give feedback on one of the darkest, most desperate moments in their life. In the past, no one ever wanted my feedback. But that was starting to change. The First Step is: "We admitted we were powerless over our addiction and that our lives had become unmanageable." In treatment, when someone does their First Step, they share the insanity and unmanageability of their disease. The spiritual principle underlining this step is honesty. It takes some serious honesty to look at yourself—the good, the bad, and the ugly (and at this point, there is mostly just ugly)—and tell the truth. *I can't stop using. I have mistreated others. I have been selfish. I am broken. I can't do it alone anymore.*

Looking around at the motley crew assembled to participate in the ropes course, I was struck by the diversity of this group. As the saying goes, "Addiction does not discriminate." There were doctors there, lawyers, plumbers, and construction workers—people who had a PhD and people who never even got their GED. But we were the same. We were absolutely the same. I saw all of the people who sat in on my First Step. I'd only known them for a few weeks, but I trusted them. They'd been to where I'd been. They had seen me at my ugliest, and, yet, they had not rejected me. They still chose to be there for me.

It was here, as we guided others through the ropes course and as others guided me, that it hit me—life is a ropes course. It is often unstable, precarious, and dizzying, which is why we need each other. We so desperately need each other, people who can help guide us through life's tricky corners, because often the things that come naturally to us are the things that eventually kill us. And so we need a voice outside of ourselves to remind us and reorient us toward our goal.

When you come to the end of the ropes course, you come to what is called "the leap of faith," where you fall back into the safety of your friends' arms. Symbolic of the many unknowns in life, the leap of faith is one where you must trust in something bigger, better, more powerful than yourself. Doing this was hard for me. The only thing I had practiced faith in over the past few years was myself. I'd needed every bit of ingenuity and creativeness just to survive. But that was the problem. I'd only been surviving. I hadn't been living. I hadn't been loving.

The ropes course reminded us we could have faith in the fellowship of our new friends. No matter how far we fell, we had a safety line that was connected to us. It wasn't until we became vulnerable as we did in the ropes course, or as we did with our First Step, that we could feel the arms of our friends—or more importantly, our God—surround us. It wasn't until we reached the end of our rope that we reached out and took the hand of God. I was starting to see this now. I was starting to experience real life.

Not everyone took the leap of faith—some because of their fear of heights, others due to their fear of the unknown or their fear of falling. Whether or not you took the leap of faith, there was no guarantee of long-lasting recovery and sobriety. But I made myself do it. I was not taking any chances. I had to do things differently this time. I had to doubt my doubts, question my questions, and live my life with faith in something bigger, better, and more powerful than I.

When I got to the leap of faith platform, I didn't give myself time to talk myself out of it. The second they told me they were ready for me, I launched backward as instructed. For a second, I thought, *How careless*, but the reality was this was one of the most careful things I had done in a long time. To listen to someone else for a change, to trust in someone other than myself for

The Ropes Course

a change, to fall, fully expecting to be caught by someone who loved me. The fall lasted only a second, but it seemed, in the anticipation, to last an eternity. But then, at last, I felt it. The arms of my friends enveloping, the grasp of my God folding me in. It almost took my breath away, this time not with the crushing weight of control and addiction but in the sheer delight of freedom. Absolute freedom. Now I could become the person God had designed me to become. I didn't have to have all the answers. I could start taking little leaps like this in life, listening to the directions of good people and trusting in the faithful catch of my God. A verse shot through my mind. "I give them eternal life, and they shall never perish; no one will snatch them out of my hand" (John 10:28, NIV). No one could snatch me from His love. No one could take me from His plan. Sure, I could ignore it and get detoured for a while, but He was the Great Shepherd. He was a master at guiding wandering sheep back to the fold. For the first time in a long time, I felt safe. Safe in the arms of my new friends, and safe in the renewed grip of my God.

Chapter 13

Family Day

On Family Day, I would see my wife, children, and parents. I had been in treatment for twenty-one days. Just one more week, and then I would head home. To stay clean in a controlled environment like this was one thing, but to stay clean after being thrust back into the world was quite another. So many questions, very few answers. But I didn't need to worry about that right now.

I sat in my room watching as cars began to arrive at the Walker Center, pulling into the parking lot. Before I completed my twenty-eight days of treatment, I had to go through "Family Day." I couldn't wait to see them, but I was afraid of what they would think when they saw me.

The people here in treatment had become my family, my confidants. They knew more about me than some of my own family. But there was so much of me that they still didn't know. Honesty had not been my policy for very long. Like a pair of jeans that haven't been worn in a while, freshly dried, it was a bit too tight and foreign to my frame. There was still too much of the street in me. The con. The manipulator. No one but God was really seeing all of me—the Richie I wanted them to see. Family Day was another step in the process of becoming vulnerable and healing.

Family Day

It was a time when parents, spouses, and kids came to see their family member who is in treatment. It was also a type of therapy for them. It gave them a chance to say the things they needed to say. I was afraid of what they would say. I was afraid my wife would say what she had every right to say: "Richie, I cannot put up with you anymore," or, "I can't forgive you for what you have done." It happens to people all the time. Why not me?

I watched as a couple of kids saw their mom for the first time in weeks. Their eyes brightened up, their entire faces turning into smiles. The father couldn't help but smile a little too. But it was a cautious smile. Too many smiles had been crushed, too many hopes dashed against the cliffs of reality.

Before too long, I saw my dad's blue Dodge truck pull into the parking lot. Inside were my mother, father, wife, and two children. My heartbeat increased as I anticipated seeing my family. What would they think? What would my wife say? Would she still be angry? Had I done irreparable damage to my children?

The truck stopped, and Brittney and my mother got out first. My breath was knocked out of me a little when I saw my wife. It was like I was seeing her for the first time. It's in moments like this that you realize how much the drugs dumbed down your senses. You cannot appreciate anything when you're high except the high itself. But after you stop using, after a few days, suddenly you start to see things you couldn't see before. Like the way my wife seemed to glow! Her big eyes looked like an ocean. I wanted to fall into her eyes. She laughed as she said something to my dad. Kaleb got out of the car next. He'd grown so much, his inquisitive mind taking in his surroundings. My mom got Hayley out of her car seat. Hayley was happy to be out after the long drive. She smiled as the sun reflected off her blond hair. A sudden pang of panic set in when I thought of seeing them. What would I say to them? What would they say to me?

I got up and walked toward the entrance so that I could see them. I passed the nurses' station. One of the recovery addicts was asking for some medicine for a headache. The pleas fell on deaf ears. The medicine given out during Family Day was extremely restricted. They didn't even give out Tylenol. Nothing. They didn't want the addicts to medicate their feelings. They wanted the addicts to be able to feel, deal with the emotions, and then finally heal.

I saw my family coming to the front door on the opposite side. We saw each other before we reached the glass door. My wife gave me a smile. It was small, but it was a smile. I hadn't seen her smile in so long. Life had not given her a whole lot to smile about. When we opened the doors, Kaleb ran up to me and gave me a big hug. Hayley, only two, recognized me but was a bit more hesitant. I melted underneath the love captured in Kaleb's hug. His age had protected him some from my addiction. I couldn't hold back the tears. I couldn't keep back the sobbing. I was so incredibly happy. This was the happiest I had been in a very long time. Brittney closed in on me and the kids, and she hugged me too. I was instantly restored in this hug. I was redeemed. It was everything I had lost in active addiction. I would never lose it again. My parents also surrounded us, crying their own tears, having their own hopes, dreaming their own dreams. "Dear God, help Richie get it this time."

I breathed a sigh of relief. My wife had greeted me with a smile and a kiss instead of a slap and some divorce papers.

"How is it going?" my wife asked.

"It has been incredible so far. It feels so good to be clean," I said. I meant it.

"That's great, Richie," my mom chimed in. "How is it compared with past treatment centers?"

"I think pretty much the same. Except now, I am actually listening." All the treatment in the world won't help someone who is not willing to listen to the prescribed plan.

"You look good," my mom said.

"Thanks. The food is pretty good. It's amazing what just eating can do for you," I said with a little smile, realizing it was too close to the truth to be funny.

I took them down the hall. Hayley was in my arms. I told them everything from my counselors' names to what we had for dinner last night. It was so good to see them. At that moment, I realized how much I'd missed them. Not just from being separated the past last three weeks but from being separated over the last few years. I'd missed playing with my children. I'd missed laughing with my wife. I'd missed being with them. Just being with them.

We went into the main meeting room where the owner of the Walker Center would meet the families and explain the day. We still had ten minutes, so I took Brittney to show her my room. The cards Brittney had the children make for me covered the walls near my bed.

"This is my room," I said. Ron was sitting at his desk. He had no family coming. "Brittney, this is my roommate and friend, Ron."

"Hello, Ron," Brittney said, taking his hand and shaking it.

"It's great to finally meet Richie's better half," Ron said with his signature Ron smile.

"He's my fellow Norwegian," I said.

"That's right. They've got to keep us rascals quarantined from the rest of the group. They don't want us to corrupt everyone else," Ron said as he grabbed his notebook and headed for the hall. "It was nice to meet you," he called back, leaving Brittney and me alone for just a minute.

She was beautiful. My sins suddenly felt exceptionally evil, ugly, and bad. In the presence of her beauty, I felt inadequate. Poor thing got stuck with such a loser. But she did not look at me like I was a loser. She did not see the junkie I had become. She looked at me with eyes that saw her husband, the man she married, whom, although the beginnings were a little rough, she loved. She smiled at me as she took me by the hand, bringing me to her and giving me a kiss. Electricity. White-hot electricity jolted through my body as we hugged each other. The first hug I remembered feeling for years. I could've lived in that hug the rest of my life.

"I love you, Richie," she said. Her voice cracked a little. "I am hurt, but I love you." She tightened her grip before releasing me. I took both her hands in mine.

"I love you, too, Brittney. And I know I've said it thousands of times, and you're probably tired of hearing it, but I am sorry. I am so incredibly sorry." This apology I actually meant. With this sorry, I wished I could go back in time and undo every bit of heartbreak I had done to Brittney. She smiled at me before saying, "We should probably go back."

"Yep, you're right." I took her by the hand and walked with her back to the meeting hall.

The room was filled now. So many kids laughing. So many couples smiling. But underneath the thin layer of mirth was pain. Heartache. Some of these addicts would be dead in a few months. Many of them relapsed. The odds of an addict making it are so slim. I looked at my family listening to the speaker; I was determined to make it this time.

Chapter 14

Give and You Shall Receive

When the orientation ended, the patients were separated from their families again. Families of addicts have their own separate group sessions. It's only a few hours for the counselors to educate the family on how the disease of addiction affects everyone who knows the addict. Some people really hate it when they call addiction a disease. They think it's the easy way out. They think you're making an excuse. They don't understand why the addict can't just quit. However, addiction being a disease does not let the addict off the hook. Only through daily medicine, like any other disease, can you arrest it and live a good life. The medicine isn't pills but prayer, honesty, hope, and accountability, to name just a few.

I waved to my wife and kids as I left the room and headed for my own group. I carried my Narcotics Anonymous basic text like a Bible. I'd never read a book that shared my story quite as much as this book, except for Bible. These books were my medicine too.

The rest of the day seemed to fly by until we came to the moment everyone had been waiting for, when the family—those who have been hurt the most—get to express that pain to you. We had been thoroughly instructed on what we could and could not do.

Darkness Will Not Overcome

"This is not about you," one of our instructors had said. "This is about your family and the pain they've gone through. You need to receive it. You're not allowed to speak the entire time. No interrupting." We weren't even allowed to cross our legs and arms or slouch. They even told us not to nod too much. Avoiding anything that could take away from the family member that was sharing their pain, probably for the first time ever, was the focus. They'd put up with our constant shenanigans, lies, manipulations, and apologies. Now it was time for us to listen. Don't hand them Kleenex, don't console them while they cry. There are, apparently, all kinds of subtle ways we can try to make this about us. As the cliché goes: feel, deal, and heal. Our families had to feel, deal, and heal like us.

Only my mom and wife would be participating in this exercise. My dad was watching the kids outside. It wasn't just us. There were about five other patients with their families in the circle too. We would be going on this roller-coaster ride together.

Brittney went first. The room was bright; all the blinds were opened wide. We were letting the light shine on the pain and lies. The instructor/facilitator reminded us of the rules before we began, and then he asked Brittney to start. Brittney gave me a small smile as if saying, "I'm sorry for what's about to happen," then began. For the next twenty minutes, Brittney shared the pain I had put her through. The constant fears for my health, the constant paranoia and worry whether I was using.

"I can't even walk out of the room without taking my purse with me," she said, moisture appearing in her big blue eyes. She shared incident after incident, broken heart after broken heart. I didn't remember doing half the things she said, but I had no doubt I did them. The past few years were nothing but a blur, with brief moments of lucidity. Missed birthdays, missed Christmases. I had been missing, like a child on the back of a milk carton, except everyone knew where I was, just not how to reach me. I realized the pain I'd caused. I realized the trauma I'd caused. Shame was sitting on my chest, bouncing, like one of my kids would if I were lying on the floor. It almost took my breath away. But I still sat there and received it. With open posture, I kept my hands on the arms of my seat, knuckles white from holding so hard. It was the least I could do. This had nothing on the pain I'd put her through.

When Brittney finished, all we could do was hug. We were not supposed to say anything. It was a delicate time. It only took one, "I'm sorry," to bring back a horde of bad memories and cause the family member to question your sincerity. So we hugged in silence, the only sound some sniffles from the circle of people sitting in the room, surrounding us. They could relate to everything just said. It brought up their own pain. It dragged their own skeletons out. It felt good knowing we were not the only ones with skeletons—skeletons that had been haunting our closets for years, hiding under our beds since some of us had been kids. It is so easy to think that you're alone. That nobody's going through what you're currently going through. We don't want anyone to think badly of the son, husband, friend we love, so we hide it and pretend nothing is wrong. But it's a lie. It is a lie that keeps us sick. You could see the relief in the eyes of everyone as they unleashed things they had been holding in for years. Feel, deal, and heal. However, not everyone found it therapeutic. There were plenty of families who walked out of the room frustrated and angry.

"Why should I have to be here? I don't need therapy. You're the one who screwed up. You're the one who has neglected our children," one of the participants yelled at his wife. He got up and left the room. The facilitator did their best to try and encourage the patient. Her fellow patients tried to look at her reassuringly. But the helplessness and loss could be seen in her eyes. She knew things would not get any better, at least for her marriage.

My mom went next, her eyes already red from tears. She didn't wait or hold back; she unleashed.

Darkness Will Not Overcome

"Richie, I am tired of living each day worried about whether I am going to get a call that you're arrested, or worse, dead. Your father and I have worried ourselves sick. We are almost bankrupt financially. We are almost bankrupt emotionally." She continued for a solid twenty minutes (the maximum amount of time given). She shared her perspective. What it was like for parents to watch their child slowly kill himself. What it was like to watch the father of your grandchildren neglect, even endanger, their grandchildren. It was hard for me to hear, not because it wasn't true but because it was. It was some of the truest stuff ever said. I once heard someone say that "humanity runs on denial like cars run on gas." We are constantly self-deceiving, justifying bad behavior, judging ourselves by our motives but judging everyone else by their actions. We're constantly giving ourselves breaks—*Oh that's just the way I was raised*—but not giving anything to other people. And this goes for everyone, even "normal people" (nonaddicts), and times ten the denial for the addict. Addiction and honesty cannot live within a person at the same time, which is why the first principle of the First Step is honesty. Everything must start with honesty. I don't care if you have a problem with heroin, smoking, lying, overeating, pride, being judgmental, enabling, you name it—freedom has to begin with getting honest. I watched as the weight my mom had been carrying around was slowly being lifted as she shared her pain, her guilt, her frustration. It hurt to say it to her son, but she had to. It hurt to hear it, but I had to listen. I had to start getting honest about all the havoc I had caused.

As my mom was finishing up, she reassured me of her love.

"Richie, your father and I love you so much. I'm not telling you this to hurt you, but to help you," she said. "We love you." She got up from her chair; so did I. We hugged for what seemed like a long time. So much significance and emotion were wrapped up in that hug. She whispered she loved me one more time to really drive home that point. But I knew. I always knew

Give and You Shall Receive

they loved me. In fact, it was because I knew how much they loved me that I exploited that. I took advantage of it, played the angles. Like we say in recovery, "You can love someone right into the grave." The bailing out of jail, hiring attorneys, constantly giving money. We want to do it for them because they're our children. However, unless the addict is ready to get clean and stay clean, all those things you try to do to help them actually hurt them. They need a deeper love than that. They need to have the type of love that lets them experience the consequence of their action. It lets them stay in jail. It lets them go through withdrawal. It lets them get hurt by the things they're doing. That's real love. It's hard to do, but it must be done. My family certainly helped me a lot. I am thankful for the attorneys, posted bail, the treatment centers. However, it is a fine line between helping and hurting, empowering and enabling. Eventually, my family discovered the balance, and so did I.

Family Day finished with us back in the meeting hall. The lead counselor took just a few minutes to thank the families for coming and reminded them of a few of the things they had learned today that were so critical. There was so much emotion in that room—regret, remorse, shame, anger, even hate. But the strongest emotion in that room was fear. Fear that when the patients got out, they'd go back to the drugs. Fear that this would fail. Fear that things would not change. Fear that, in the end, you'd end up alone.

After the final meeting, I walked my wife and mom outside to my dad's blue Dodge truck. I ran up to Kaleb and Hayley and picked them both up.

"I've missed you guys so much," I told them, smothering them in kisses. "I can't wait until I get home and we can play together." Kaleb's eyes lit up. Hayley continued looking at me inquisitively. But she recognized me. Maybe, for the first time, she saw her father, the one that was deep down inside of me, stifled by my using. I hadn't been clean more than a few days since she had been born. I had missed so much. I was determined not to miss any more!

I squeezed them one last time. My father, who wasn't able to be in the meetings, hugged me.

"Richie, please just stop," he said, having a hard time articulating his feelings. "Just please stop. We don't want to lose you." A tear rolled down his cheek that he quickly wiped away.

"I know, Dad. Thanks for everything."

He smiled and then got in the car. Final hugs and goodbyes. It wouldn't be too long before I saw them again, at least Brittney. I was coming home in a week. One more week left, and I would be back home.

Chapter 15

Graduation

On the day I graduated from the Walker Center, it was hard for me to believe I'd made it through twenty-eight days clean. This was the first time I had gone that long since I started using. Twenty-eight miracles. Twenty-eight, twenty-four-hour periods of freedom. I could sleep now. I felt good when I got up now. There was still that deep hunger for the dope. There was still that feeling of grieving a missing friend or family member. But now I realized it was a friend or family member that was lying to me and slowly killing me. So I would continue grieving them until I no longer remembered them, until they were no longer the main thing on my mind.

We were all sitting around in a giant circle as we did for our groups. Looking at each other. Being accountable to each other. Seeing the good, the bad, and the ugly in each other. My NA basic text was being passed around. As was the custom, people were signing it; people were writing little notes to me in it. I'd known these people for only a short time, but I had been more open and honest with them than with most everyone else. We had a common goal. We had a common problem. We had sought each other out in order to help fill in the broken spaces of our lives. I would read these notes for years to come. In moments of

Darkness Will Not Overcome

worship and devotion, during times of difficulty, I would be led back to where my journey began. I would be reminded that "I may not be where I want to be, but at least I am not where I used to be." I would remember the day God spoke to me, and I finally listened. I would remember my friends from the Walker Center, their faces appearing as I read their little notes to me:

Richie, I love you dude! I can't tell you in words how incredible it has been to be here with you. I wish you nothing but freedom from your addiction and to pursue a wonderful life which will include blessing others just because you are there. Stay in touch.—Matt

Richie, it's been a pleasure and an honor to get to know you. I wish you nothing but the best. But you can only receive the best by staying clean. I know you can do it. Remember that at the times of weakness that you are not alone, for God loves you! Remember, 1 Corinthians 2:9 says, "No eye has seen, no ear has heard, and no mind has imagined what God has prepared for those who love him" [NLT]. Love, Jim

Richie, take care. Enjoy one day at a time and one step at a time. Don't fall, but if you do, I will be there to help pick you up.—Big Mike

Richie, it has been a real pleasure knowing you for the last three weeks. Your calmness and pleasantness are extraordinaire, along with your knowledge. Buddy, you've got what it takes this time; stay focused, concentrate, I believe in you. Love you man!—Phil

Richie, you are a cool person. You've been a real leader to this group. Everyone respects you and there will be a big

GRADUATION

void when you are gone. I wish you and your family all the best. Be good to yourself.—Mary

It has been quite the experience. I have watched you change from a young man who was beat up, and still beating himself up, to someone who is overflowing with confidence and self-worth. I cherish the time that I got to spend with you, and look forward to future conversations. Your family is lucky to have you as a son, husband, and father respectively. I hope this isn't goodbye. Love you man.—Mike

Richie, you helped me so much in our discovery. I can't believe it is almost over. You have so many blessings and support from people that love you. Your friendship has meant so much to me. I think you are a humble and good person that walks with God. You have a gift. Remember that. I will never forget you even with my meth head. Thanks for everything. I will pray for you. Love you always.—Bryce

Richie, thanks for all the memories we shared at the WC. It has made it so much easier for me to be able to laugh a little. You are a very special person. You always speak from the heart. Thank you for sharing your First Step with me. It helped me a lot to look deeper at my own addiction. Thanks also for being there during my First Step and offering words of wisdom and encouragement. I love you, man! So may God be with you and good luck in the future.—Brian

Richie, do not ever lose the glow in your eyes that you have right now. Always remember how it feels.—CB

I believe in you, my friend. I know you will live. Just don't let dust get on this book.—Ron

Darkness Will Not Overcome

Tears appeared in my eyes as I looked up from the book to the people's faces. They were far kinder to me than I deserved. But that's what people need when they start out on this journey. They need to celebrate the small steps. They need to rejoice over one day of being clean. That may not seem like a big deal to most people, but to addicts, it's massive. Those words of encouragement would do more for me than these people would ever know.

The counselor began speaking, reminding us that treatment is worthless if we don't practice what we've learned. He looked directly at me and said, "Richie, you have got to put a lot of work into your recovery. You worked every day on your addiction. You sacrificed everything for it. If you want to stay clean, you're going to have to sacrifice for your recovery. It doesn't just happen. If you used every day, you're gonna have to pray every day. If you used to lie every day, you are going to have to get honest every day. If you conned and manipulated every day, you're going to be accountable and tell on yourself every day. The past twenty-eight days will have been just one big waste of time if you don't leave here and go to twelve-step meetings."

I nodded my head. I had heard this speech before, or one like it, all the other times I had been in treatment. But this time, I listened to it. There's a big difference between hearing something and listening to it. For the first time in a long time, I listened.

The counselor got a coin out of his pocket—the ceremonial graduation coin. Every time someone graduated, we gathered in our big circle, passed the coin around to each person, and gave our prayers for the person while holding it.

"Lord, help _____ stay clean this time."

"Lord, enable _____ to live a new life."

"Lord, help them!"

"Lord, heal them!"

"Salvage their life, salvage their brains, salvage their marriage."

The prayers varied from person to person. However, they all could be summed up in one phrase. "Save me." The cards were

Graduation

stacked against us. The statistics on recovering addicts are not good. As I had already discovered, relapse was a very real and common thing. The only problem for the addict relapsing is that their life is on the line. Many addicts never make it back after a relapse. And so we prayed our prayers for the person as the coins came around. Much of ourselves were in those prayers. As we prayed for the graduate to make it, we were also praying for ourselves to make it. When we prayed they would cling to God more, we were praying that we would cling to God more. We fused our hopes and fears and dreams not to the coin but to the person the coin represented. We asked the God of the universe to step into their life/our lives and change them/us. Save us! Save me from giving up or giving in. Save me from losing my temper and acting out in my anger. Save me from my impulse to go to the drug when the going gets tough. Make me turn to you instead of to the dope. Make me the father, the mother, the son, the daughter, You originally intended me to be. Help me find a job. Help me keep a job. Save me from the penitentiary. Save me from myself. Lord, save me!

My mind goes briefly to the scene in the Bible when, for a moment, Peter walked on the water. For a moment, Peter experienced the exhilaration of participating in a miracle. He walked on the water. For an addict, to stay clean is a miracle. It is walking on water. It is not doing what comes naturally (using) but, rather, trusting in God. It didn't take long for Peter's humanity to get involved; he started looking around and became afraid. Matthew 14:30 says, "But when he saw the wind, he was afraid, and beginning to sink he cried out, 'Lord, save me.'" That is an addict's prayer if there ever was one. Save me! Keep me from drowning. Keep me from falling. So many waves. So many worries. So many things I have no idea how they will pan out. At that moment, you start falling. Everyone one of us has fallen. Every person in the world has fallen, and so we cry out like Peter, "Lord, save me." It has to be a quick prayer, not a long one with fancy words; you'd end up underwater before you got the prayer out of your mouth. It only takes a second to sink under water. It only takes a second to sink under life. So the prayer has to be fast. It may not be fancy, but it's effective. It needs to be practical. You can't get more practical than calling out, "Lord, save me." Save me from my stupidity. Save me from my ego. Save me from my impulse. Lord, save me. That is the prayer I prayed for every person who graduated before me. And that was the prayer I prayed for myself

As the thought of leaving the Walker Center, a safe place, began to overwhelm me; as the thought of the warrants for my arrest waiting for me back home started raging and the bills on the kitchen counter started intimidating me; just like Peter, as I started to sink, I prayed, "Lord save me," and just as with Peter, "Jesus immediately reached out his hand and took hold of" me (Matthew 14:31).

Chapter 16

Reunions

I saw my wife first. Brittney was waiting for me by the baggage claim. Kaleb and Hayley were with her. She smiled when she saw me. Her smile shot life into me. She pointed Kaleb and Hayley in my direction, and Kaleb ran to me. I couldn't hold back the tears. All the emotions held at bay for years now rushed through my body.

I grabbed Kaleb and picked him up. He felt lighter than usual, or I was stronger than usual. He saw the tears. He was not used to seeing me cry, but he was old enough to understand that these were good tears. Hayley was still hiding behind her mom, watching me from behind her legs. I ran up to them, gave Brittney a kiss, and then squatted down to bring myself to Hayley's level. I played peekaboo with her for a few seconds, tickling her sides with my fingers. She giggled, and I grabbed her, covering her with kisses.

I put my arm around Brittney and scooped up Hayley. Kaleb trotted along, telling me every story and thought that came to mind. I felt complete. So absolutely complete. My heart felt fuller than it ever had. But there was still something in the back of my mind. There was still the hunger to use. I was still grieving the loss of one of my closest friends—a bad friend, one that was killing me—but one that was a significant part of my life no less. I quickly played the tape all the way through and pushed the side of using away. You can't give it any thought. Otherwise, it will begin to take over your thoughts. The hunger was still great, but my love for my family and the presence of my God were much stronger.

We got into the car. Brittney asked me whether I wanted to drive. I reminded her that I still didn't have a license. My license had gotten revoked over the last year.

"Oh, that's right," she smiled. We laughed about it a little. The thought of all the things that I had to deal with entered my thoughts. I missed a court hearing when I was in treatment, which meant there was yet another warrant for my arrest—a failure to appear warrant. One thing after another. Not to mention everything else I had to do. But I reminded myself, "One day at a time. One step at a time." The clichés really worked. They were vital to keeping your head in the game and out of trouble. If you focus on the stack of bills, how people are going to react, what they're going to say, or the question, Am I going to end up in jail? it becomes overwhelming. If things become too overwhelming, the temptation is to go back to the one thing that will make all the problems go away, at least for a few hours. But I had seen through the lie. I knew the right choice now.

Brittney and I talked like we did when we first dated, back when we first got to know each other. In some ways, we were just getting to know each other again. I had not been myself in years. Kaleb jumped into the conversation anytime he saw an opening. When my thoughts began to drift, I brought them back to the now. I was sitting with my family, something I had not been able to do in a long time. I realized how much I had taken for granted. Finding peace and joy in the little things is what makes life worth living. Sure, the big things are great: graduations, a new job, a new child, a new house, and so on, but it's in the little day-to-day things that real living happens. Living life with the ones you love.

Reunions

We drove home the usual route, a route I had driven a thousand times. But now, it looked different. Everything looked different.

"We've really missed you, Richie," Brittney said.

"I've missed you guys so much." I was sure there was a part of Brittney that wondered whether that was really true.

Yeah, if you really missed us, why would you have kept using? Why would you have kept stealing? If you really missed us, why would you have put us through so much hell?

However, if she thought it, she didn't show it. Thankfully, Brittney's hope and love for me outweighed the pain and distrust. She really believed and hoped that I would make it, that we would make it, that we would live together in holy matrimony. In sickness and in health. Well, she had definitely stuck with me in the sickness part. Now I hoped we could experience the "in health" part.

Over the coming years, it wouldn't all be easy. There would be plenty of times when the anger and resentment of the past would come up. When people get clean, they often fall into the trap of thinking that their family should just open their homes, their hearts, and their wallets for them. They should trust them. As I would discover, trust takes time to earn back. I had stolen from Brittney and our family so many times in the past, it would take time to trust me again. During those early days of recovery, I had to get rides everywhere I wanted to go. I had to ask for money. No one made me grovel, but the reality is that trustworthiness builds over time. I had to understand that being clean for a few weeks does not erase years of abuse, neglect, and hardship. Over the coming days, weeks, months, even years, it took time for the wounds of addiction to start to heal. But our love for each other was stronger than our dysfunction. I would come to discover that very few marriages make it after the abuses of addiction. It was by grace that I was blessed to have one that did.

The car pulled into the gravel driveway of our small farmhouse.

Darkness Will Not Overcome

With it came so many memories from my days of using. The barn I often used in. The places I hid my drugs. The places I smoked. But in those moments when my mind kept returning to the bad times, I would look at my wife, I would look at my children, I would look to the sky and remember it wasn't all bad. This area could become consecrated, holy ground again. I could live here without living the nightmare of the past few years. But I would need godly people in my life and to depend on God like never before.

I read a book to my children and put them to bed, their soft skin and peaceful rest easing the weight of life for a moment. I saw one of the letters I wrote to them pinned to Kaleb's bed. My pitiful attempt at drawing a hippopotamus made me smile. I read the letter.

Dear Kaleb & Hayley,

I miss you guys so much!
I think about you both all the time. I can't wait until I can see you again. We will play all day. Kaleb, you and I need to work on our fort again. I miss working on it with you! When I get back, we will do whatever you two want to do. We can go to the park and fly a kite, you name it, the sky is the limit for us. Please kiss your mother for me. Give her a big hug. Kaleb, you're the man of the house while I'm gone. Be a big boy for me. I love you guys!

P.S. Here's a little poem I wrote about you both when you were babies:

> Hollow, drum roll, on your tummy makes us
>   both laugh.
> I never knew someone was capable of loving
>   someone like I love you.

REUNIONS

Your eyelids wave like palm branches of peace,
Your lips, like rounded petals, whisper new
 creation.
Your coos make me cry,
Thank you, God, for giving them to me,
For entrusting their life with my life.
"Fragile, handle with care."
I will. I promise I will.

—Dad

Chapter 17

Recovery

I walked into the Twelve Step meeting, found a seat, and sat down. Brittney had dropped me off and would come back for me after she finished her errands. For a moment, I resented my situation, getting dropped off and picked up like a kid. But then I pushed it out. I reminded myself this was one of the consequences of my actions. It would get better.

I had committed to attending ninety meetings in ninety days. That meant a meeting every day for the next three months. I needed it. I had used drugs every day. I had stolen every day. I had lied to someone every day. I needed to do this every day. It kept me centered. It kept me humbled. It kept me focused. It was a huge inconvenience to Brittney to have to drive me to meetings every day. However, it would be an even greater inconvenience if I started using again.

There are all kinds of different people at twelve-step meetings. Doctors, lawyers, construction workers, black, white, poor, wealthy (although the wealthy rarely make it into the room before they've lost all their wealth). As one of our mantras says, "It doesn't matter if you got your education from Penn State or the state pen. Addiction does not discriminate." The beauty of twelve-step meetings is that they remind us that no matter how different we look or what our backgrounds are, under the surface, we're all the same. We bleed the same color of blood. We dream the same dreams. We're all like Humpty Dumpty, broken people looking for someone to help put us back together again. We're put back together again by each other. It's why it is called a fellowship. What we could never do alone, we can do together. We're put back together by God. Many of the people who end up in a twelve-step program meet God for the first time in these meetings. These twelve steps carry us from the bottom of the barrel back to some semblance of normality. The practical lessons from the steps are very much like the ones I was taught as a kid except they're written in a way that is good for addicts. It cuts through the fancy words and gets to the heart of what we need. Honesty, faith, hope, surrender, trust, to name a few—all things I desperately needed.

I sat down in the circle of chairs and looked around. What a motley group of misfits. We had found our home. We had found a place where, some of us for the first time, we really belonged and could get better. I recognized one of the people who came in. He had been at many of the meetings I'd been to. His name was Marvin. He was five feet, nine inches tall, and was almost as wide as he was tall. He had a huge beard, drove a Harley Davidson, and had a tattoo on every visible part of his body. He looked like a pretty rough dude, but whenever he talked, he spoke with a gentleness and kindness that I wanted for my life. He always seemed happy, which was something I wanted too. He didn't seem to lose it at the drop of a hat, which was also something I wanted. I wanted him to be my sponsor.

A sponsor is someone who has something that you want. They have some clean time and some recovery under their belt. They've worked the twelve steps and will help guide you through them. They have a sponsor who has a sponsor who has a sponsor. They're a mentor to life. And Marvin was the guy I wanted to be my sponsor. He looked nothing like me. His background was very different from mine. But we had something in common. Something more significant than anything else. We both wanted to live a happy life, free from the prison of addiction.

The meeting started. *A newcomer is the most important person at any meeting because you cannot keep what you have unless you give it away. Get a sponsor. We are totally self-supporting, not accepting outside contribution.*

There were some newcomers at this meeting. I was glad I'd been coming for a couple of weeks and no longer had to identify this as my first meeting. Most meetings with newcomers become a meeting on the First Step. People share their stories. *No advice. Don't talk about something you don't know. That'll get someone killed.* So I just kept my mouth shut. I'd been clean for only a couple of months. What did I know? So I sat and listened.

The meeting continued with the usual stories of bitter ends and new beginnings. However, my mind kept drifting to asking Marvin to be my sponsor. Why would a biker want to have anything to do with a pastor's kid from suburbia? But I'd put a lot of thought and prayer into this. Marvin was the one. They tell you not to be hurt if the person you ask to be your sponsor says no, but let's be real. If Marvin said no, I was going to feel like an idiot. I didn't really know why, other than the fact that I didn't do well with rejection.

The meeting came to an end. We circled up, holding each other up, and recited the serenity prayer: "God grant us the serenity to accept the things we cannot change, the courage to change the things we can, and the wisdom to know the difference. Amen." Such a simple prayer, but so significant. It has brought me back to sanity more than a few times. I can't change what I have done, but I can change what I am doing. I can't change my spouse, but I can change the way I react to her. I can't change my boss, but I can change the way I let him get under my skin. So many things I tried to control with the drugs—my feelings and my outcomes. Control, control, control. However, I was starting to experience the freedom that comes when you see how little control we really do have. I could let God do His job, and I could focus on mine. I had learned to stop wasting time and energy on what I had no control over so that I could spend more time and energy on what I did have control over. Serenity, what a beautiful thing! The peace that passes all understanding.

The prayer ended, and people let go of each other. People disembarked from the safety of the circle into the wide-open world with its scary decisions and painful emotions. However, we knew we could succeed now; what we could not do alone, we could do together. People laughed, hugged, and started saying goodbye. There was a reassuring lightness in the room. No pretense. We were who we were. We were not excusing it, but we were not lying about it either. It was nice to be able to be yourself for once.

I went up to Marvin. He was in the parking lot, getting on his bike.

"Hey, Marvin, I'm Richie."

"Hey, Richie. I've seen you around for a couple of weeks. How's the recovery going?"

"It's going pretty good," I said.

"Good. Keep coming back. It really does work when you work it."

"I was wondering—" I suddenly second-guessed myself. Maybe this wasn't such a good idea—

"If I would be your sponsor," he finished my sentence.

"Actually, yeah. Would you?" I was about ready to go into the speech I'd prepared for this moment when he continued.

"Call me every day for the next thirty days, and we'll see how it goes. All right? Even if it's just to call and say, 'Hey, I'm doing all right.' We don't have to have some long conversation on the phone. It's just to keep everyone accountable and develop some healthy habits," he finished.

"Absolutely." My eagerness for mentorship was obvious. I was desperate for someone to help me learn how to live life clean.

Darkness Will Not Overcome

Marvin put on his helmet. He started backing up his bike a little.

"It really does work if you work it," he said, and then pulled out of the church parking lot and went down the road. I could still hear that signature Harley Davidson sound even after I no longer saw him.

I forgot to ask him whether he wanted me to start calling him that night. I would call him, just to be safe. I was so desperate to stay clean, and I was scared to do anything that might sabotage it. I would've stood on my head if they told me to stand on my head. It's ironic. It was out of desperation that I started using drugs, and it was out of desperation that I had reached a point where I would do anything in order to stay clean. You have to be desperate enough to step out of your comfort zone. You have to be desperate enough to try something you've never tried before and talk to people you wouldn't regularly talk to. You have to be humble, and life had humbled me. Life had brought me to my knees, but it was on my knees that I had started praying. It was on my knees that I had felt the calming presence of God's Spirit. It was on my knees that I had found the strength to stand up tall for what I should be doing and to stand up against what I should not.

A cool breeze blew through my hair while I stood outside, in the parking lot, waiting for Brittney to pick me up. There was a little bit of spring in that breeze. Just a tiny piece of warmth reminding me that winter was coming to an end. *Thank you, God, for reminding me that my winter is coming to a long-anticipated end.* I saw our van heading in my direction. Brittney pulled up. I couldn't wait to tell her that I had a sponsor, someone other than her to help me in my journey.

Chapter 18

Judgment Day

I showed up at the courtroom in Nashville early because my wife had to drop me off before she went to work. It was a beautiful spring day, but I didn't appreciate it because I was worried about what would happen. It was the day of my court hearing. Judgment day had arrived. Each police officer that walked by me made my pulse quicken. I was waiting for the one that would throw me to the ground and cuff me. Of course, none of them did.

I was as prepared for this as I would ever be. I had been clean for two months. I'd been working on my twelve steps with Marvin. We had even gotten together last Sunday with a group of our sponsorship family. A sponsorship family, or tree meeting, is a get-together with all the people sponsored by a particular person. Randy was Marvin's sponsor. This meeting was with everyone Randy sponsored and all the people they sponsored. It was only a couple of hours, eating together and sharing what was going on in our lives. It was an incredible experience. In addiction, you lose the gift of having a good time without the aid of some type of mood-altering drug. You start to believe the lie that you can't have fun without it. I was starting to see through that lie. I had started laughing again—real laughter. I had started to cry again—real tears. In addiction, I always felt alone, but in recovery, I recognized all the people who cared about me. In addiction, you only look out for yourself, but in recovery, you look out for others. When it became my turn to share what was going on in my life, I shared what was weighing most heavily on my chest—my court hearing. Would I be going away to the penitentiary? The feedback I received from the group was good, but it was honest. Basically, put it in God's hands and what will be will be. "If God brought you to it, He's going to bring you through it." Now that I was standing at the doorway of the courthouse, I had to lean on every single word of encouragement that the fellowship had to give.

I saw my attorney coming up the steps. I breathed a sigh of relief. I'd had the same attorney since the beginning. This was not my first showing in court. However, this was one of the more important ones.

"Hello, Mr. Halversen," my attorney said.

"Hello."

"How have you been doing?" He didn't come out and say it, but I knew what he wanted to know. Was I clean?

"I am doing good. I celebrated two months clean the other day. I've been working a twelve-step program. I have a sponsor," I said. I saw immediate relief in the attorney's eyes. This was the first time we had gotten together, and I had good news for him.

"That's great. I am glad to hear it. More importantly, the judge will be glad to hear it," he said as he opened the door for me. "This is what's going to happen. We're going to let them know you're here and then they are going to arrest you." He saw the fear in my eyes. "You have a failure to appear warrant for your arrest. So this is standard procedure. They will arrest you and take you back to a holding cell where all the other inmates are being kept. That's where they will keep you until your name comes up on the docket, at which point they will bring you out before the judge. I will be out here waiting for you. As long as everything

Judgment Day

that you're telling me is true, everything should work out fine."

We walked into the courtroom; it was bustling with activity. Attorneys talking to attorneys. Family talking with family. Attorneys talking to clients. We went to one of the bailiffs, and my lawyer let him know that I had a failure to appear warrant. The bailiff looked over the docket for the day, found my name, and then told me he was going to arrest me.

"Your hands, please." He put handcuffs on me and escorted me to a back door and led me through. I looked back to my lawyer for a second, wondering whether this was going to be the last time I saw him, wondering whether I would be going away for a long time. The guard led me to a back room and motioned to another guard, who opened the door. The lock clicked, and the guard opened it. The room was filled with inmates. There were no seats. It would be standing for me. I didn't care. I was so nervous that I wouldn't be able to sit anyway.

A few minutes went by, and suddenly I heard my name. Not from a guard this time but one of the inmates. I looked in the direction my name was called from. At first, I didn't recognize anyone. And then I zeroed in on David. David was someone I used to buy drugs from. David grew up in the same church and attended the same school as I did.

"David, what's up?" I asked. I realized how stupid it was to ask that almost as soon as it was out of my mouth.

"Well, as you can see, nothing much, man. What are you doing in here?" he asked, making some room beside him so I could sit down. I sat down.

"I have a court hearing. I missed my last hearing due to being in treatment, so I had a warrant for my arrest." I didn't have to ask David why he was where he was. I already knew. A drug deal had gone bad. Someone got shot and killed. He was being tried for accessory to murder. I had gone to school with this guy. We ran in the same circles. Suddenly it hit me—I was fortunate that I was not in the same situation he was in. He was just in the wrong place at the wrong time. How many times had I been in the wrong place?

"Treatment, eh?" he asked with a touch of skepticism.

"Yeah. It wasn't my first time. But I am hoping it was my last time."

"I hope, for your sake, it does work. I have my doubts, but different strokes for different folks, I guess." David wasn't yet ready to recognize he needed help or that he had a problem. He still thought it was all just a matter of bad luck.

"Yeah, thanks."

"Do you have any cigarettes?" he asked under his breath.

"No, sorry. I'm actually trying to quit." His disappointment was apparent. He probably already regretted he made room for me beside him.

"How's your family?" I tried to change the subject.

"They're good, as far as I know." David had a young son. My wife's family was very close with some of his family. "As you can imagine, I don't get to see them much."

We sat there in silence for the next thirty minutes. Very few people were talking to each other. Most were sitting in quiet dread of what might happen. I stood up and walked over to the small, three-inch-wide, three-foot-tall window. I saw cars drive by. I saw people walking by. It's in moments like these that you realize how much you take for granted—just the freedom to walk where you want to walk and drive where you want to drive. Just the freedom to step outside and enjoy the sunshine. I made a vow to never again take that stuff for granted. I would enjoy every beautiful day, even every not-so-beautiful day. At least I was alive and free. I whispered a prayer to God.

"Father, forgive me for squandering the life You gifted me with. Please forgive me for taking it for granted. I promise I will never take it for granted again. I will treasure the moments. Not just the big moments but the little moments. The walks outside. Laughing, crying, and playing with my kids. Thank You

Judgment Day

for giving me my life back. Thank You for helping me appreciate the small things again. If it's Your will, Lord, I pray that I might get out today. But if not, I will still trust in You. I have made my bed; now it's time for me to sleep in it. Thank You, though, for Your mercy. For all the beds that I made, but instead of making me sleep in them, You slept in them. Thank You that where my sin increased, Your grace abounded more. You have been so good to me, in spite of me. Thank You, God. Thank You for everything." Only a redeemed life can still praise God in a prison cell. It is by sheer grace that I was going before the judge over prescription fraud charges and not something like David, accessory to murder. "There, but for the grace of God, go I."

Thirty more minutes went by as I looked through the sliver of window. And then I heard the door open and a group of names being called. My name was one of the names called. I headed for the door. I nodded to David as I walked by. He barely nodded back. I didn't hold it against him. No doubt, he had more on his mind than how polite and friendly he was being to me. In prison, there's no time for social graces.

The guard guided us back to the courtroom. All the inmates sat in one section. I was the only one in our group who was not wearing an orange jumpsuit. I hoped it stayed that way.

When my name was called, I went and stood with my attorney.

"Richard Halversen, you have three felony charges of prescription fraud. Also a failure to appear for your court hearing. Why did you miss your hearing?" The judge looked at me with piercing eyes.

"Sorry, Your Honor. I was in treatment. In Idaho. I should have notified you, but I wasn't thinking straight. I just needed to get to treatment. I felt like it was a life and death situation," I responded.

"Did you finish the program?" she asked.

"Yes, Your Honor. It was a twenty-eight-day program. I have been going to meetings every day since. I have a signed record of my meetings." The judge had the bailiff bring the meeting list to her.

She took a moment to look at it. She peered up from the paper seconds later and asked, "Are you clean?"

"Yes, Your Honor, I am. Over two months clean." I couldn't hide my pride. I had not been two months clean for a very long time.

My attorney said some things to the judge, some law lingo I didn't quite understand, but basically requesting a later hearing and asking that I might still be able to be released on bond. The judge did not respond immediately. She just looked at me for a moment.

"We will drug test Mr. Halversen, and if he comes up clean, we will continue to allow him to be out on bail. If he's not clean, he's going to be staying in jail until his next hearing. Mr. Halversen, make sure you make your next hearing."

After the pound of her gavel, my attorney and I went downstairs where the drug test would be administered. I took the drug test, and of course, I tested negative for the four main drugs they tested for. I could leave. Free. Well, not completely free yet, but thankfully, I was going home. I was going to be able to put my kids to bed tonight.

My attorney told me what would happen next and then said goodbye.

"Goodbye. Thank you for everything." I realized how blessed I was to even have an attorney, an advocate, even if he was paid to do it. At least you have someone in your corner pulling for you. I had seen the difference between people who had an attorney and those who did not. It was significant.

I went to a pay phone and called Brittney to tell her the news. She was happy her husband would not be going away to jail today. She did not get off work for a few more hours. I would have to burn some time in Nashville. There was an NA meeting in West End, a few miles from me. If I left now, I should be able

Judgment Day

to make it there before it started. I headed in that direction.

It was a beautiful spring day. It was even more beautiful now that the weight of wondering whether or not I would go immediately to prison had been lifted from me, at least temporarily. The air smelled just a little bit cleaner. The sun was shining just a little bit brighter. My step was a little lighter. I heard the hustle and bustle of the city, but it did not drown out the beauty of nature. I saw a squirrel run up a tree. A cardinal was sitting on top of a branch, singing, each realization an announcement of my recovery. I thanked God for my freedom.

Thank You, God, for the freedom to go for a walk on this beautiful spring day. To not have to worry about getting high, and how I'm going to get high, and how I'm going to get the money in order to get high. In addiction, I was never able to appreciate walks like these. Thank You for giving walks back to me—thank You for giving my life back to me.

A huge smile filled my face as I said *Amen*, the word many people use to end their prayers with. It is a Greek word that means "truly." Truly, I had been given my life back. Truly, I had been reborn. Truly, I was able to enjoy life, enjoy my wife, enjoy my children. I hadn't been able to enjoy those things for such a long time. But "truly, amen," I was able to now. *Thank You, God. Truly.*

I looked down at my watch and then quickened my pace. The meeting would be starting soon. I should be able to make it. If I was a couple of minutes late, that was OK. I had already started my own meeting, walking in West End during a beautiful spring day, more free than I'd ever been before.

Chapter 19

Making Amends

I was sitting in my car outside a dentist's office. This was a place I had been many times before, but this time it was for another reason. This visit wasn't to get drugs but to make amends for the headaches and hardship I had caused this particular dentist. I had impersonated him, for years, to call in my own prescriptions. How many times had he been wakened in the middle of the night, interrupted during his vacations, infringed upon during his family time, because of my selfishness? The pharmacy didn't always call to confirm, but many times they did. The shame of what I had done overwhelmed me to the point that I didn't want to get out of my car.

I had been working the steps with Marvin and had made it to the infamous ninth step, "Make direct amends to such people wherever possible, except when to do so would injure them or others." In the eighth step, you make the list of who to make amends to. This had taken months; I still had people come to mind that I had to put on the list. So many people hurt by my selfishness. You realize early on in the steps that it's not a quick and easy process. It is a simple process, but by no means easy. I would be working through the steps for the rest of my life, each time dealing with a new defect, attitude, or habit.

Making Amends

I stepped out of the car and made my way toward the office door. I had written a letter to Dr. Smith several weeks ago, just asking whether he would be willing to meet with me. He knew immediately who I was. The step work was clear. You make "direct amends, except when to do so would injure them or others." I was included in "others." Making amends didn't mean putting yourself in harm's way to make things right. There were some amends you had to make from a distance. There were even some amends I had to make posthumously. Some people died before I could speak to them, not to mention the countless people I hurt through the ripples of addiction that I had no idea I hurt. With those unique situations, I have had to go to God and leave them with Him. Some people write a letter to the individual/individuals and then burn it up. Others have met with their family. The key is that you make restitution as best you can.

I contacted another one of the dentists that I had impersonated, and he was clear. "I don't want to ever speak to you. You are a piece of garbage. I do not waste my time with garbage. I don't care if you are clean. I've been clean my whole life. I don't see me getting a reward for that," he said in his return letter to me. When making amends, you get all kinds of different responses. That's OK. The key is that you did your part. The amends is about setting you, and the victim, free from the pain from the past. Even when someone does not accept your amends, you have done your part, and you experience the freedom that ensues.

I opened the door to the doctor's office. It was lunchtime, so he had no appointments for the next hour. This was the only time he had. I let the receptionist know who I was, even though she knew already.

"I will let Dr. Smith know," she said. She disappeared into the back. My heart was beating out of my chest. I kept reminding myself that though this was hard to do, the joy and peace I would have from this step would be well worth all the uncomfortable feelings I had to feel. I was not here just to say, "I am sorry."

Darkness Will Not Overcome

Family and friends of addicts hear *sorry* so much it becomes a hollow word. They hear it so many times they stop believing it and start resenting it. You steal some money out of their purse and get caught. "I'm sorry." You're late to your kid's birthday party. "I'm sorry." They pick you up at the jail. "I'm sorry." You forget your anniversary; no, you don't just forget your anniversary, you take money from your wife on your anniversary. "I'm sorry." Very quickly, "I'm sorry" doesn't cut it. When I was in active addiction, Brittney got so tired of hearing me say "I'm sorry" that one day she turned to me, staring squarely into my glossy eyes, and said, "Richie, you are sorry." She was right. Sorry was simply used when no other lies or deception could be used. It was a sorry attempt of easing things over until you got caught again. Thinking back at some of my sorry attempts at saying "I'm sorry" makes me cringe.

Since being in recovery and working the steps with Marvin, I'd discovered that "making amends" does *not* mean saying you are sorry. It is so much more than that. It's putting things back to rights. It's not only apologizing for the behavior but also stopping the behavior, and it is making restitution for the behavior. Making amends for stealing is giving the money/item back and no longer stealing. The amends for an explosive temper is not just saying "I'm sorry," it's apologizing for the behavior, it's listening to any pain the person has been holding on to, and it's no longer acting out in anger. In the case of Dr. Smith, I was here to express my apology for all the pain I had caused him and to ask whether there was anything I could do to repay him.

The receptionist returned. She smiled at me and invited me to follow her back to Dr. Smith's small office.

"Hello, Mr. Halversen," Dr. Smith said with a genuine goodness I did not deserve. His eyes reflected only kindness. I was expecting to see resentment.

"Hello, Dr. Smith. Thank you so much for taking time out of your busy schedule to meet with me just for a few minutes."

Making Amends

"Sure. I was glad to get your letter. I am glad you're doing better."

"Thank you," I said, and for a second nothing else came out. What do you say? How do you start? And even though I swore I was not going to start with "I'm sorry," I did.

"I'm sorry, Dr. Smith. What I put you through was awful. I took advantage of your trust and your good name."

Dr. Smith just listened. The kindness in his eyes never left. I remembered the definition of *amends*, to "compensate or make up for a wrongdoing," and I said, "Is there anything I can do for you, or give you, that can make up for some of the pain I've caused you?"

"No, Richie. This is enough. I forgive you." The words breathed new life into my life. The growing weightlessness of life just grew lighter. I can't think of anything more freeing than the words *I forgive you*. Real forgiveness. He didn't just say it and then return to treating me badly; that's not forgiveness. He looked at me in a way that was new. Nowhere in his eyes did I see anger or resentment for what I had done.

"I don't know what to say," I told him.

"Don't say anything, Richie. It was a painful year. But the person I see today is very different from the person that came to my office a couple of years ago. I am glad you have gotten the help you need."

We sat and spoke for another thirty minutes. He asked questions about my family, my job, my life. He told me about his life. We spoke to each other as though we had known each other for years.

When the time came for his next patient, I said goodbye and left. I left with such a load lifted that I felt as though I were walking on air. As I was driving home, I realized the importance of this ninth step. Freedom is found in forgiveness. Regardless of how the people I was making amends with reacted, I was being set free by the simple act of making things right. Whether I received the reaction I wanted or not, the freedom and peace

Darkness Will Not Overcome

from this step ensued. I didn't have any control over how people responded, only the way I responded. And for today, I didn't want any hard feelings holding me down. I didn't want any of the past holding me back.

Paul writes in 2 Corinthians 5:17, "Therefore, if anyone is in Christ, he is a new creation. The old has passed away; behold, the new has come." If you want to *be* a new creation, you have to *live* as a new creation. It means doing things differently. It means learning new things. It doesn't happen by accident. If you only want to know what you already know, you're severing yourself from the new life God promises to us. This goes for everyone—not just addicts. He promises, "Behold, I am making all things new." "Behold, I am doing a new thing" (Revelation 21:5; Isaiah 43:19). If you want to live a new life, you better plan on learning a few new things along the way.

Chapter 20

New Life

As I write this chapter, today marks three years clean. But not just clean. Recovering. Each day I am becoming a better person. I am learning how to live and cope with life as a recovering addict.

Today is also special because I am graduating with my degree. Early in recovery, my sponsor, Marvin, told me to write down some goals I would like to achieve in one year, five years, and so on, of being clean.

"Don't limit God. Dream big. If you would like to see it in your life, write it down," Marvin said. "I promise you, when you look back over this, you will see that you shortchanged God in what He can do."

So I did what he asked. I wrote down everything I could think of. I dreamed big; or, at least, I thought I did. In fact, I wrote down a few things I knew would be virtually impossible. But Marvin was right.

My goals for one year being clean were things like staying clean, holding a job, and staying married, all of which God has blessed me with. Not only did I stay clean that first year, but I also helped others stay clean. I gave back to my community. Not only did I hold a job, but God also opened up opportunities I

Darkness Will Not Overcome

thought would be impossible. Not only did I stay married, but God also blessed us with another child, Tristen Patrick Halversen.

Now, three years into my five-year plan, I have achieved all the things I listed, and more. I have been able to achieve far more by living a life of recovery than I ever could have done in addiction. All the bridges I thought I had burned, I realize now that God can repair. I never thought I would get my degree. A few years ago, I didn't think I was going to live another year. But God rescued me by using a lot of special people in my life.

I lined up where the instructors told me to. Three hundred people were graduating. I never thought I would be one of them. I examined my program, fanning through until I came to my name under "The College of Arts and Letters" Bachelor of Science in Communications. I had to look back several times to make sure I was not dreaming.

We walked out at our cue, our red robes flowing, and sat in our designated spaces. So many onlookers in the audience. I searched for a while until I spotted my wife, Brittney, and our children, Kaleb, Hayley, and our three-year-old, Tristen. Tristen is the first child I've been able to experience while I was completely clean, from his delivery through the present. It has been incredible.

Sitting beside my wife and kids were my parents. Sitting beside them were Brittney's parents. They were proud of me. It was a new experience for me. It meant so much to make people proud instead of ashamed. Much easier, too, in the long run.

The president got up and began speaking. It was a message about accomplishment, new beginnings, and courage. It was a message I could relate to in so many ways—more than I think he intended. Over the past few years, I had seen so many miracles. So many things I thought were broken and beyond repair, I had watched as God had fixed each one. God fixes our mess-ups better than we ever could. Every single one. He'd taken me from someone who couldn't go a few hours without getting high

NEW LIFE

to someone who was simply high on life. It sounds cliché and stupid. But it's true.

The auditorium was like my new life: filled with hope, filled with dreams and aspirations. I had plans now. Oh, the simple beauty of having something to work toward other than my destruction. I never thought I could cope with living sober, but it is a far better experience than the best high I ever experienced.

They began calling names. I followed them as they went in alphabetical order. Before long, they came to the *h*'s. I went and stood in my designated space up near the stage. I looked at my family as I headed toward the front. Their smiles reflected my own. One of their dreams was coming true too—not that their son would get his college degree but that I would live and that my calling would find me, that I would reach my full potential—as a citizen, a father, a husband, but most of all, as a child of God. I heard my name called, "Richard Halversen," and I moved across the stage to where the president was handing out degrees and congratulating the graduates.

"Mr. Halversen, congratulations," he said.

"Thank you," I replied as I kept walking to exit the stage. Such a brief moment, but one I hold on to. It lasted only a few seconds, but it had pieces of eternity in it. It represented so much more than just a college education. It represented a new life. It represented second chances. It was proof that God really can pull people back from the dark, broken places of the world—back to the light. The light really does shine in the darkness, and the darkness has not overcome it (John 1:5).

Graduation came to an end with the usual cap toss. My family found me on the auditorium floor. We hugged. I was congratulated. Tears of joy were shed. We went out to eat together, telling stories and laughing over dinner. Such a beautiful day. *Thank You, God, for such a beautiful day.*

Chapter 21

Preacher Man

It was Saturday morning. The Sabbath. My first service at my first church as a pastor. We were still in the process of moving; my family and I came down Friday evening and stayed in a hotel, and we would head back to Tennessee to finish up the move the next day.

I looked out at the church congregation. Another surreal experience. Another dream I had thought was shattered, but God had made it possible for it to come true. Things happened so fast after graduation. I had two interviews, two opportunities on the table: one in sales in a health-care communication company—something similar to what I had been doing—the other, to be a pastor in Montgomery, Alabama. I thought back to how this all came about—a simple conversation with a friend.

I had met Chris at a restaurant. Chris and I went way back to the fifth grade. I had not seen him or spent time with him much while I was in active addiction. I didn't have time for anyone then. And so I was making up for lost time. There was a lot of laughter that evening. There always was when Chris was around.

Chris shared with me what he had been doing over the past summer—auditing for the Gulf States Conference where his father worked. The Gulf States Conference was a regional headquarters for the Seventh-day Adventist Church. His father was a part of the leadership and one of the people responsible for hiring. I didn't intend to ask Chris about any openings at the Gulf States Conference. I just wanted to make up for lost time with a dear friend. But as Chris was talking, I did ask, almost in passing.

"Hey, do you know if Gulf States needs a communication director?" I asked.

"I'm not sure. I can ask my dad for you," Chris responded.

"Yeah, that would be cool," I said.

I proceeded to tell him about my interview in Washington for the health-care communications company. But something compelled me to ask about doing communications for the church. I didn't ask anything about pastor positions. I didn't have the theology degree. I didn't believe it was possible. So I didn't mention it. But deep down, that's what my heart was telling me to do.

I remember, as a young man growing up, the son of a preacher, that's what I wanted to do. I wanted to be a preacher like my dad. But at some point, the dream started to fade. The voice from the call got softer. I realize now it didn't go anywhere, but I had started to cover it up. To cover it up with other things I thought were much cooler. But now the voice was back, and louder than ever.

The evening came to an end. Chris and I went our separate ways, and the idea of becoming a pastor disappeared almost as quickly as it appeared. But the next morning I got a phone call from Chris's dad. "Chris told me you feel called into pastoral ministry."

I was speechless. I never said anything about feeling called into ministry; at least, I don't think I said anything. I felt it; boy, did I feel it. But I didn't say it. Somehow, Chris heard it. God allowed Chris to hear what I was really praying for but too scared to ask for.

"Yes!" I declared.

"Richie, we would love to have you come down to the office and meet with us."

"Absolutely. When?"

"As soon as possible," he said.

We continued talking for a couple more minutes, finalizing a time that worked for everyone. I would do anything to make it work. It was two days after my interview in Washington, but I knew this was what God had called me to do. I kept running away from the call, but God is relentless. He continued to pursue me.

I went to both interviews. Both went well. Both offered me a job. The sales position would make considerably more money. But I already knew pastoral ministry was what I needed to do.

On the flight home from Washington, I wrote down a prayer to God:

Dearest Lord,

Thank You for my new life. Thank You for these new opportunities. Thank You for the offer from Conner Communications. But Lord, my heart is in pastoral ministry. It is deep down what I have always felt called to do even when I was too afraid to admit it. Lord, if You open this door and call me into pastoral ministry, I will go forward and won't look back. I have already squandered too much of my life. I'm not squandering anymore.

Love, Richie

As I was returning home from the interview with the Gulf States Conference, Mel Eisele, the conference president, called me and extended the invitation for me to pastor Montgomery First in Montgomery, Alabama. I said yes.

Now I was sitting in front of the congregation. As I was getting ready to deliver my first message, a small part of me was thinking, *What in the world are you thinking? What could you possibly say to these people?* But then I remembered that God had given me a message to share with others. A message of hope.

I once heard someone say that every pastor basically has just one sermon. Sure, they preach on different verses, but the central message is always the same. As I got up to begin preaching, my mind went to that first night at the Walker Center, when I heard the voice of God say to me, "Richie, if you go out that door, you will die, but if you surrender to Me, I will use you for My glory." He did everything He said. He always does everything He says. He took a drug addict, broken and empty, and gave him hope. He took me from nothing and made me something.

Chapter 22

The Darkness Will Not Overcome

Walking on the beach barefoot. The cool sand contours to my feet. I leave my imprint wherever I walk. My family and I have spent the entire day in the water. Taylor, our newest addition, runs toward me, picks up a handful of sand, and throws it at the ocean. It is a dramatic throw but falls quite short of its goal. He does not care. He is impressed. I pretend as though I am impressed too. I pick up Taylor and throw him into the air. He giggles. I cannot help but smile, completely captured by this uncorrupted son of mine. I set him down and chase him on the beach.

"Dad, catch," Kaleb yells as he hurls a football in my direction. I catch it and throw it back to him.

"Over here," Tristen shouts. I throw the football to him next. He throws it to Hayley.

Taylor comes to me and asks for the ball in typical two-year-old fashion: hands outstretched and calling out, "Mine, mine, mine." I have never felt as good as I do in this moment. My entire family is together and in one place. I am truly happy.

Brittney walks up beside me and takes my hand. She smiles at

The Darkness Will Not Overcome

me. Her smile speaks volumes. We have been through so much together, so much pain. But we have learned to forgive each other and to live in an attitude of forgiveness. Marriage does not work unless you live with an attitude of forgiveness. It has not been easy; addiction leaves a lot to be forgiven. Not only the addict but the entire family is hurt. Addiction hurts anyone it comes in contact with. Addiction hit my family with all it had. No one came out unscathed. It has not been easy. Brittney has had to get as much help as I have. She's had to deal with some of the issues in her own life. That's the problem with addiction: it can bring out the worst in a person. There have been times, I am sure, that my wife felt like giving up. There have been times that I felt like giving up. But we didn't—and that's what matters. We stuck with each other, even at times when we were incredibly hurt by each other.

We continue walking down the beach with the sun setting behind us. Golden light stretches across the ocean, setting the waves on fire. It reminds me of an experiment I once did in school as a child.

"A flame doesn't have a shadow," our teacher said. He took us to the janitor's closet—the only room in the school with no windows. We crammed in, all eighteen of us. He turned off the lights and then lit a match. He then turned on a flashlight and pointed it at the match. He was right. Flames don't have shadows. The shadow of the match was there but no shadow of the flame. Light has no shadow. It reminds me of John 1:5: "The light shines in the darkness, and the darkness has not overcome it." The darkness tried to overcome me. It almost did. At times, darkness was all I could see. But God's glimmer of light never left me. I discovered that in the moments that feel darkest, God is the closest. The moment I surrendered to God, His light overcame the darkness. It's pretty simple, but not easy. As Marvin always told me, "Don't confuse simple with easy."

Freedom doesn't happen overnight. It happens one day at a

Darkness Will Not Overcome

time. One good decision at a time. With each square inch of my soul that I surrender to God, I burn that much brighter for Him. If you hold on to the light, the darkness will not overcome you. For years, I thought God was repressive, that if I really wanted to burn brightly, I had to leave the safety of what I was raised believing. I thought that freedom meant having no rules. Now I realize that freedom is found in finding the right rules. The irony is that I left the teachings of my faith because I thought they were keeping me from living an original, exciting, life. But my departure led to the most drab, predictable, boring existence I could live—OK maybe not boring, but certainly miserable. I couldn't enjoy my children; I couldn't enjoy my wife; I couldn't enjoy life. The very things I did to "experience life" started siphoning my life away, one bad decision after another. There's nothing original, or enlightening, about addiction. It is actually very predictable because it always leads to jail or death. But God rescued me from my darkness. He has set my life on fire. I realize now that the most original, exciting, unique lives, the ones that burn brightest, are the lives of those who live the way they were designed to live.

The burning sun continues melting into the sea as the laughter of my children brings a smile to my face. I'm not worried about who I once was, except to remember that I don't want to go back. I am a new creation in Christ. God's grace has set my life on fire. No more shadows are haunting me. Flames don't have shadows. I will keep the light of Christ burning in my life for myself, for my family, and for the world. Set me on fire, Lord. I want to burn brightly for You. The darkness will not overcome.